hope lifts

STORIES OF HOPE THAT WILL LIFT YOUR SPIRIT!

RUTH CHIRONNA

Hope-Lifts: Stories of Hope That Will Lift Your Spirit!

by Ruth Chironna and others
copyright ©2017 Ruth Chironna

Trade paperback ISBN: 978-1-943294-69-5
Cover design by Mario Hood

Hope Lifts is also available on Amazon Kindle, Barnes & Noble Nook and Apple iBooks.

Contents

4

Foreword

GENUINE HOPE IS FAR FROM WISHFUL THINKING. IT IS A confident expectation linked with a yearning and desire that finds its foundation in the certainty of the promises of God as revealed in Scripture. Someone once said biblical hope is not a "hope-so"; it is a "know-so."

Long before Edward Mote was a preacher, he had been a cabinet-maker for 37 years. While he had been baptized at 18 years of age, his journey to the pulpit involved a 37-year apprenticeship with the Great Carpenter of Nazareth until, at 55 years of age, he was prepared to build and fashion the people of God to become a habitation of God in the Spirit. One morning in 1834, at 37 years of age, Mote was stirred to write a hymn between his walk to work and his evening time of sleep.

You know the opening lines of this famous hymn quite well:

My hope is built on nothing less
Than Jesus' blood and righteousness;
I dare not trust the sweetest frame,
But wholly lean on Jesus' name.

The hymn, as you now realize, is "The Solid Rock." Our hope is in Christ who is our Solid Rock! Our assurance is rooted in what the writer to the Hebrews tells us in Hebrews 6:18:

... by two unchangeable things, in which it is impossible for
God to lie, we who have fled for refuge might have strong
encouragement to hold fast to the hope set before us (ESV).

Those two things that are unchangeable are that God has sworn by an oath, and that He cannot lie. God is not one who can deny Himself even when we deny Him. The fact that God cannot deny Himself is an amazing revelation of His unquestionable and unchallengeable strength and power. You and I break promises more than we care to admit. We are fallible; we are works in progress, moving toward perfection, and yet on this side of the consummation of the kingdom we have not yet arrived. We are continuing to press toward the mark of that heavenly prize in Christ Jesus.

Christ Jesus is our horizon of hope! When we look toward the horizon of our life, our dreams in God, and yearnings for what He created us for, we see Christ. He is the One who began this good work and will indeed by His faithfulness bring it to completion. We fix our eyes on Jesus, our sure hope, and He is our powerful pull into His glorious future that continually lifts us up to higher places by calling us as He called John the Revelator to "come up higher" (Revelation 4:1). When John heard the command to ascend, to be lifted up, the Spirit immediately lifted him up into the heavenly arena and he saw that there was indeed a throne at the center of the universe, and the One who was seated on that Throne is the God of all hope, who fills us with all joy and peace in believing (Romans 15:13).

My wife has collected an entire series of stories about hope. Many of them are about people who, like Abraham, have had to "hope against hope" (Romans 4:18). These are designed to lift your spirit up into fresh hope in both God and His precious and magnificent promises.

Take time as you read these stories, these "Hope Lifts" to feel, empathize, identify with, and take strength from the hope that the Spirit quickens in your heart as you experience the hope in the words you read. Those words are not mere words, they are hope-filled words born of real-life stories that God is telling through some of your brothers and sisters in Christ, in order to encourage you to honor your own story and experience your own "Hope Lifts."

Dr. Mark J. Chironna
Church On The Living Edge
Mark Chironna Ministries
Orlando, Florida

Dedication

To my grandchildren, precious Ariana, creative Mark and gentle Londyn. My prayer is that as you grow and forge out your own journey in life, you will discover over and over again that when you hope in God, He will never disappoint. Your NiNi loves you, and so does Jesus!

Acknowledgments

THIS BOOK NEVER WOULD HAVE BEEN WRITTEN IF NOT for the seer/prophet, Bob Hartley. He gave me a direct word from the Lord about writing a book on hope during a conference in California. As I stepped out in obedience and began to collect stories of hope from precious men and women around the world, my excitement grew and I realized that God was up to something bigger than me. I believe this book will serve as a catalyst for those in need of their own personal hope-lift. So thank you, Bob, for your obedience in delivering the word of the Lord. Mark and I love you much and are honored to call you friend!

I would like to thank Carol Bailey for all her hard work in helping me as I gathered the many stories and sorted through them all. She worked tirelessly and her joy and encouragement along the way kept me going. Thank you, Carol! You are the best!

I would also like to thank Donna Scuderi for helping with the final editing. You indeed are a gift and a blessing to me! Thank you, Donna! You are loved and valued!

Above all I would like to thank my heavenly Father, for without His faithfulness and loving kindness, we would indeed be without hope.

Introduction

WE ARE LIVING IN A TIME WHEN THE PRESSURES OF THIS WORLD seem to leave us feeling hopeless. Many of us feel the stress of family challenges, financial struggles, limitations in our employment, and even political unrest. It seems that just yesterday—or maybe it just feels like it was yesterday—life was so much easier. Family values were clearly defined, and you knew that when you finished your education, a job awaited you to bring the financial security that you desired. Your future was laid out and secure.

But with the rapid pace of change, both positive and negative, taking place all around us, that feeling of optimism about the future can all too easily be replaced with a feeling of hopelessness and pessimism.

But then the question arises, is God still in charge? Does He really know what is going on in and around us, or are these challenges taking Him by surprise? Does He really hold the world in His hand or is the tension in the nations catching Him off guard? Well, if we know the living God who created this world and holds it together by His Word, then we know that He is still in charge and nothing catches Him off guard. Our very steps are ordered of the Lord. Jeremiah 29:11 says, *"'For I know the plans that I have for you,' declares the Lord, 'plans for welfare and not for calamity to give you a future and a hope.'"*

The Lord has plans for each one of us! That word *plans* in the Hebrew refers to thoughts, intentions, purpose and imagination! Our heavenly Father not only knows the purpose and intention He has for our lives, but He has activated His imagination in forming those plans! Just think about that! Our Papa has dreams and wishes for us! And those dreams and wishes are for our *welfare* and not for *calamity*. They are for our peace and well-being. His plans are not for affliction

13

and adversity. They are not for distress or evil. His plans give us a *future and a hope*!

If the enemy of our soul can take away our hope, he will take away our future. It's our future in God that he is after. The way to prevent us from walking out the plans God has for us is to take away our hope! That is why hopelessness is so prevalent among people of all ages. Not only does the Lord have plans for us, but the enemy has plans for us as well. His plans are to *steal, kill and destroy*. The enemy would like nothing more than to steal your hope by killing God's plans for your life and ultimately destroying your future. His plans are to bring death, whereas God's plans are for life.

I recently had a significant dream that brought to light just how deeply this feeling of hopelessness had taken root in my own heart. I would like to share it with you because it may minister to you as powerfully as it did me.

In my dream, I was responsible to care for a number of small children. Along with a few other adults, we brought our group of children to a large, dark castle where they would be babysat. When we went back to retrieve the children, we found that the caretakers were horribly evil and had dismembered the limbs of some of the children and had killed and buried some of the others. Some parents who had placed their children in these people's care simply never found their children again and had no closure as to what had happened to them. When all of this came to light, I felt it was my responsibility to keep all the children safe and away from these evil people.

With this sense of purpose, the scene in my dream changed and I found myself in a large classroom filled with hundreds of students. I remember being surprised that the students ranged in age from small children to adults, but they had all been placed in my care. The students were very unruly, and I quickly began to establish the rules for the classroom. As I was doing this, I woke up.

I knew this dream was significant and prayed for the Lord to help me interpret it. I immediately sensed that the evil people who were killing the children and dismembering them were three demonic spirits—fear, unbelief and pessimism—that were seeking to kill the "children" being birthed in me in the spirit. The children represented my hopes, dreams and visions for my future. Like in my dream, I knew that I needed to protect what God was birthing in me in the spirit.

I began to meditate on the three demonic spirits of fear, unbelief and pessimism. I knew from being taught on dream interpretation that the Lord was showing me these were feelings, emotions and spirits that I was personally wrestling with. I realized that I had allowed myself to become distracted by the cares of this world. I was concerned about the economy and the state of our nation. I began to take my eyes off the faithfulness of God and was looking for solutions to come from the government. When I did not see any coming, I allowed fear, unbelief and pessimism to enter my spirit. I began to lose hope for the future.

I realized that I was not the only one who was wrestling with these feelings. Many in the Body of Christ, as well as people in secular society, were wrestling with the same sense of hopelessness. The Holy Spirit began to show me that the enemy was using a cord of three strands (fear, unbelief and pessimism) which could not be quickly or easily broken. These were becoming strongholds in the minds of many people. But God never leaves us without hope! Whatever the enemy throws at us from his kingdom of darkness, God has the answer in the kingdom of Light! He began to show me His cord of three strands which cannot be quickly or easily broken—love, faith and hope!

The Word declares: *"There is no fear in love; but perfect love casts out fear..."* according to First John 4:18. So when I hide in the love of my heavenly Father, all fear has to go! Love will drive it away!

When I allow faith to work in me, unbelief cannot stay. Hebrews 4 tells us that unbelief causes hardness of heart. I had to repent for allowing my heart to become hardened with unbelief. I had to make a decision to believe that we serve a God who cannot lie, and that every promise He has made shall come to pass! There is a rest of faith that we can enter into when we deal with unbelief.

The last strand of the enemy's threefold cord is pessimism, and that can only be overcome when we find our hope in the Lord. Psalms 42:11 says, *"Why art thou cast down, O my soul? and why art thou disquieted within me? hope thou in God: for I shall yet praise him, who is the health of my countenance, and my God"* (KJV).

We serve a faithful God whose desire is to show us His incredible love and ignite our faith and give us a hope that cannot be disappointed! It is for this reason that I have set out to write this book on hope. My prayer is that the One who has incredible plans for you will minister hope to those areas in your life where hopelessness seems to have the upper hand. With this in mind, I have compiled actual modern-day stories from people just like you who have faced seemingly hopeless situations, and have seen the God of Hope intervene on their behalf. I have called their stories "hope-lifts" as I desire that their stories of hope will lift your spirit, as they have mine. May you be refreshed and restored as you read their inspirational stories.

And I would like to start this journey by sharing my hope-lift with you. Let's begin...

Hope for the Barren One

"'Shout for joy, O barren one, you who have borne no child;
break forth into joyful shouting and cry aloud, you who have
not travailed; for the sons of the desolate one will be more
numerous than the sons of the married woman,' says the Lord."

—Isaiah 54:1

MY HUSBAND, MARK, AND I WERE MARRIED IN 1979 and, like any newly married couple, were deeply in love and excited about the future. That future included our hope of expanding our family by having children. In 1980, I found myself pregnant, and we were overjoyed. Shortly thereafter, I miscarried and found that I could not become pregnant again. We went through the usual things an infertile couple goes through; it included many trips to different doctors trying to determine the cause, much prayer and plenty of tears. All of it seemed to no avail.

In the meantime, we became involved in full-time ministry. In 1988, we planted our first church in Raleigh, North Carolina. One of the purposes for building our church was to see God raise up a house that modeled racial reconciliation. This had yet to be done in Raleigh. Shortly after we started the work, I was cleaning my house when the Lord clearly spoke to me. Now it was not an audible voice, and I daresay I am not one to claim that God clearly speaks to me on a regular basis. But without any shadow of a doubt, I knew God spoke to my heart and asked me if I would be willing to adopt an African-American baby.

This stopped me in my tracks for a number of reasons. First of all, I was praying for a child, but up to that point I had not considered adoption. Second of all, I had never considered having a child of another race. I considered for a moment some of the social ramifications of that decision and responded to the Lord saying, "If that is what You have for me, then I say yes." After that, I let the idea go and continued believing God for a child.

About a year later Mark was conducting a leaders' meeting at the church when he stopped what he was sharing and told the men that the Lord had just spoken to him. He shared that the Spirit of God told him that we were going to adopt a biracial boy and that he would be a sign to the city that God was bringing the races together. Two days later, we received a phone call from a fellow minister saying that there was a little boy just born in another state who needed a home. The boy was biracial; his birth mother was Caucasian and his birth father was African-American.

Mark declared, "That is our son!" God did an absolute miracle by connecting us with an agency in Raleigh that pushed through the necessary home study, and we brought home Matthew when he was three months old! Now, if you know anything about completing a home study, you are aware that the process takes over a year. God moved on our behalf, and we were able to complete the initial process in record time. *Matthew* means "gift of God," and that is exactly what he has been to us! He is now happily married with three beautiful children and involved with us in the ministry.

Ephesians 1:4-5 says: *"In love He predestined us to adoption as sons through Jesus Christ to Himself, according to the kind intention of His will."* The Father, through the finished work of the cross, has adopted us all. God may not have given me a baby the way I thought He would, but He does all things well! I could never imagine my life without my sons!

I am sure you noticed that I just said *sons* and not *my son*. Well let me share with you how that all came about!

About a year and a half after adopting Matthew, Mark and I felt it was time to begin looking to adopt another child. We had considered adopting a girl, but every door seemed to close. It seemed that God had something else in mind. The agency that helped us with our home study was doing their best to find us another child. After a few failed attempts, they came to us and said that they had a little six-week-old boy who needed a home. After seeking the Lord, we decided that we would indeed adopt him, and were excited that God was adding to our family. Matthew had just turned two and was thrilled with the prospect of becoming a big brother.

Things seemed to be going as planned with our new arrival until Daniel turned about seven months old. It was at that time that we noticed that he was not progressing at a "normal" rate. He cried a lot, but the pediatrician assured us that it was just colic. But when the time came for him to be sitting on his own and turning over, Daniel did neither. We pointed this out to the doctor on one of our regular visits. He shared our concern and sent us to a specialist, who in turn began to run a battery of tests. All the tests came back negative, but we still had an infant who was not developing. As Daniel grew, he began to crawl by remaining on his back and arching his neck to scoot across the floor. The doctor told us that he believed Daniel would never walk and probably not live beyond five years old. He added that if he would ever walk, he would first have to roll over on his right side, which up to this point Daniel had never done.

We were devastated by the news and cried out to God for a miracle. We knew that unless God intervened, the situation was hopeless. We did everything we could in the natural. This included following the directions of a nutritionist and predigesting all of Daniel's formula by running it through a yogurt maker so his body could absorb it. We also took Daniel for physical and oral therapy. This process went on for a full year, and still Daniel was unable to sit up, crawl and speak, much less walk.

When Daniel was close to two years old, Mark and I went to a large conference where he was one of the evening speakers. We left the boys at home with a couple from our church. The meetings were incredible, but the truth was that our hearts were burdened for our little boy. After Mark ministered, he began to share about our struggles with Daniel and the doctor's grim report. He told the people attending the conference how the doctor said that if Daniel were ever to walk, he first had to roll over on his right side and crawl.

Oral and Richard Roberts were in attendance that evening. When Mark was finished speaking, they came to him and said that while he was sharing about Daniel, they both had a sensation go down their right arms and believed that God was about to do a miracle for Daniel. We took hold of that word and believed for just that. When we got back to our hotel room later that evening, we had a message from the couple that was watching the boys. We called them back and they could hardly contain their excitement. They said that earlier that evening, Daniel had tucked his right arm under his body and had been crawling around the room ever since. We asked them what time it happened, and as you can already guess, it was exactly the time that Oral and Richard felt the sensation in their right arms. We knew we were seeing God perform a miracle in little Daniel's life!

Daniel began to progress and grow stronger, but had yet to walk. A few months later in prayer, Mark had a vision of little Daniel in a green velvet shorts outfit with a white shirt, green bow tie, white socks and white shoes. He was sitting next to me on the front row of the church in the vision. Mark then saw himself raising his hands and giving the benediction. What he saw next had yet to happen: He saw Daniel jump off the front seat and walk up the steps of the platform into his father's arms. Mark held this vision in his heart and believed that God would indeed complete what he had begun in Daniel.

I was unaware of the vision my husband had and went shopping one Saturday for the boys' Sunday outfits. Daniel was two years old by now and still had not walked. I bought him a green velvet short outfit with a white shirt, green bow tie, white socks and white shoes. I dressed him in the outfit that next Sunday morning. I sat him next to me on the front row for the service. At the conclusion, Mark raised his hands and began giving the benediction. Daniel jumped off his seat, walked up the steps to the platform, right into his father's arms! Needless to say, we all had church! God performed a miracle right before our eyes—and it was exactly the way Mark saw it in his vision!

A few days later, we brought Daniel back to the specialist who had previously told us that Daniel would never walk and not live beyond five years old. This time, however, Daniel walked into his office holding onto the hand of his father. The doctor saw us come in and asked Mark who that child was. We told him it was Daniel and he said that was impossible.

Well, in the natural it was impossible, but with God nothing is impossible! He took a situation that was absolutely hopeless and performed a miracle! Not only did Daniel walk when the doctor said he never would, but he did not die before age five, either! Daniel is now twenty-one years old and about to graduate with his associate's degree in film and editing.

We serve a miracle-working God who can bring hope to the seemingly hopeless!

—*Ruth Chironna*

Hope for a Miracle

"When the day came that Elkanah sacrificed, he would give portions to Peninnah his wife and to all her sons and her daughters; but to Hannah he would give a double portion, for he loved Hannah, but the Lord had closed her womb....She, greatly distressed, prayed to the Lord and wept bitterly. And she made a vow and said, 'O Lord of hosts, if You will indeed look on the affliction of Your maidservant and remember me, and not forget Your maidservant, but will give Your maidservant a son, then I will give him to the Lord all the days of his life'.... It came about in due time, after Hannah had conceived, that she gave birth to a son; and she named him Samuel, saying, 'Because I have asked him of the Lord.'"

—*I Samuel 1:4-5; 10-11; 20*

I WAS MARRIED ON SUNDAY, NOVEMBER 1, 1953, AND FOR OUR honeymoon, we went to Washington, D.C. On Tuesday evening, November 3rd, my husband came out of the bathroom while I was getting ready to go to bed and said to me, "I think we should get a divorce." I said to him, "Are you crazy? We just got married!" I then I asked him what made him say that. He replied, "I don't think I can father a child." I told him not to think about that. Later on he told me that he had been injured while on maneuvers in the army.

The following day, we went on a tour of three different shrines. The first one was a Roman Catholic church that was in the final stages of being built; the second was a Protestant cathedral that was also being built; and the final one was a Franciscan monastery. When the bus arrived at the first one, we viewed the sanctuary, and then we went downstairs where chapels were being completed in memory of loved ones. I recalled what my husband told me the prior evening, and I said to myself, "I am going to pray in this place as God is God and He will hear my prayer whether I am at home in my own church or here in this one." I got on my hands and knees and prayed this prayer, "Father, if I do become pregnant, I will dedicate the baby to you, whether it is a boy or girl." Nine months later, I gave birth to a beautiful baby boy.

In 1986, my husband had to undergo a double hernia operation. My son, his wife and I, went to the hospital to see my husband while he was in the recovery room. I went in first, and then my son and his wife went to see him. The doctor was in the room when they went in. The doctor told my husband the operation was successful, but expressed his sympathy over the fact that he was sterile and unable to have children. My husband told him to tell that to our son who was standing right there!

At the age of nineteen, my son was apprehended by the Lord and has been serving Him mightily in full-time ministry for over forty-three years!

—Alba Chironna

Hope for the Brokenhearted

"He heals the brokenhearted and binds up their wounds."
—Psalms 147:3

MY FIRST MARRIAGE WAS NOT HAPPILY EVER AFTER, AS some would hope. Two weeks before I was to say, "I do," I knew that I shouldn't get married. I felt that gut feeling we all have felt at some point that warns us that we are about to make a wrong choice. But being young and naïve, I ignored it.

One evening, a year later, as I hustled to get home from a long day at work, I heard the most devastating news. When I stopped by the babysitter's house, a longtime friend of my husband's, I was asked by her boyfriend to talk with him outside for a minute. It felt awkward that he needed to talk to me outside, and my heart began to race as we stepped outside. He informed me that my husband was cheating on me with our babysitter for quite some time. I broke into a million pieces and my heart fell to the floor. My head was spinning in circles. I couldn't even speak. It had only been a year into our marriage. How could this happen to me? I didn't understand. How could he allow me to go into her house every day, drop off my son, and speak to this woman as if nothing was wrong? Completely distraught, I took my son and rushed to my mother's house—the only place I knew where I could find comfort.

When I reached my mother's place, I could hardly breathe. I buried my face in my hands and wept for about an hour. The pain ran deep; it was almost unbearable. At this point, my husband didn't know that I found out about the affair, but my mother didn't seem startled by the news. She opened up and began to share that she and my father had suspected him of having affairs even while we were dating. I wasn't angry with her, but my anger was directed toward my husband completely! I hated him and wanted a divorce.

My husband and I argued that night and every night that followed. There was nothing in me that desired to fight for my marriage, and the thought of finding love, peace or joy seemed hopeless. My marriage was over, and while he continued to have affairs, every part of me was continuously breaking and drowning in a sea of despair. I asked myself daily what I had done wrong, and I wondered if I was even worthy of true love. I started to go to church with my mother and rededicated my life to Christ.

One of my good friends, who encouraged me during this time, invited me to her church one Sunday. As I was getting dressed to go, my husband walked into the house, and we began to argue until we both decided to walk out. He drove off on his motorcycle headed to some bike event, and I headed to church. Angrily I drove, trying to calm down with the determination not to let my painful marriage stand in the way of my relationship with God.

At the end of the service, the pastor gave an altar call. At first, I didn't feel like going up, but the pastor kept walking through the aisle, calling for someone to come. There was a stirring in my heart, and I decided to go forward for prayer. Immediately the pastor spoke to me and said that God wanted me to stop arguing. He said that my life was never going to be the same from that day forward.

I was so happy! I thought God was going to turn around my marriage. Yes! This is what I wanted! After church, I stopped by my mother's house for lunch, and we shared our experiences at church that morning. Around 3 P.M., I received a phone call from a detective who said that my husband had been in a tragic accident. I didn't understand all that he meant and wasn't prepared for what would come next. On my way to the hospital, I saw his motorcycle on the highway surrounded by several police cars, and the road was blocked off. I felt in my heart that this was not just a simple accident. It turned out that he was dead on the scene.

I didn't know what to feel. I cried, but it didn't seem real. I felt as if I was outside of my body, observing what was happening. I was a single parent overnight. Alone! I was reminded of the word God had given me that morning; that my life was never going to be the same. At that moment, I knew that God was with me on this journey. I was never alone. He comforted me during the dark hours of realization that my husband was gone. He comforted me during those angry hours when I felt as if he had left never really understanding how much he had hurt me and broken my spirit. I decided on the night of his funeral to stop by the former babysitter's house. I asked her to come outside to talk. She did, and I said to her, "I forgive you and release you."

A year later, I felt God calling me to attend Bible college in Rhode Island. The challenge of being away from family and friends in New York, being a single parent starting over, and being alone was overwhelming. It was then that God was able to take me on a journey to heal my heart from the deep wounds of my loss. It was painful. During this time, God revealed to me that I struggled with anger and bitterness. I realized that I never even mourned the death of my husband. I was so angry, controlling and untrusting because he hurt me and left me alone.

The journey of healing was long, but because of God's love, freedom came in and I was able to release the pain. I struggled in another relationship during that time but don't regret it because through that relationship my inner pain was healed. I learned during that time that God loved me unconditionally. God was healing me so that I could be ready for a new journey...a new love...and a new me!

—*Natalie Wilds*

Hope for Healing

"'For I will restore you to health and I will heal you of your wounds,' declares the Lord...."

—Jeremiah 30:17

THERE ARE TIMES WHEN GOD ALLOWS CIRCUMSTANCES TO arise in our families when we need hope. Such was the case for me.

Without any prior symptoms, my husband began to have pain in his side. Our doctor was gone for the weekend, and my husband decided to wait until the following Monday to make a visit. During the examination, it was discovered that he had a serious gall bladder problem and was immediately sent to the hospital. On the way there, I prayed that God would intervene on his behalf and all that was needed would be for the gall bladder to be removed. However, while on the operating table, the doctors discovered that gangrene had set in, which could ultimately lead to his death.

But God had other plans for his life! My husband fully recovered and did not require any further medical attention. God had indeed performed a miracle! His life was spared so that he would see his four children grow up and share with me the blessing of seven grandchildren. We indeed serve a mighty God!

—Elise Paulsen

The Hope for a Child's Healing

"But Jesus said, 'Let the children alone, and do not hinder them from coming to Me; for the kingdom of heaven belongs to such as these.'" —Matthew 19:14

I AM BLESSED, HAVING BEEN RAISED IN A LOVING CHRISTIAN home with three other siblings. I was the middle girl, but a bit of a tomboy growing up. I loved the outdoors and enjoyed playing sports.

One day I was playing stickball outside and decided to see how far I could bat a large rubber ball. I threw the ball in the air and pulled the bat back for a forceful swing. When the bat hit the ball, instead of the ball going forward, the bat bounced off the ball and came back around and hit me in the jaw. The pain was immediate and intense. Because I knew that nothing was broken, I didn't go to the hospital or even tell my parents because I was embarrassed. As the day progressed, the pain intensified in my jaw and it hurt to chew or move.

We were raised in church and went to Sunday school every weekend. I remembered my teacher telling us the story of Jesus healing the man born blind and telling him to go and wash in the pool of Siloam. When the blind man obeyed Jesus, his sight was immediately restored. When I took my bath that night, I recounted that story and with childlike faith I decided that if Jesus could heal that blind man by washing in the pool of Siloam, He could heal my painful jaw as I washed in my bathtub. So I remember asking Him to heal me. I then scooped up some water in my cupped hands and, washing my jaw, I commanded the pain to go. Immediately the pain left and I was completely healed!

—Anonymous

Hope for the Impossible

"And he said, The things which are impossible with men are possible with God." —Luke 18:27 (KJV)

IT WAS MAY 27, 1987. IT STARTED OUT LIKE ANY OTHER DAY, but it soon turned out to be a day that I would remember forever. At 1:45 a.m., my husband, Tom rushed me to the E.R. at Winter Park Hospital. I had a severe headache and had become disoriented. My brain was swelling and my vital signs were unstable. Our family doctor came in and informed my husband that they were uncertain as to what the cause was, but they would have a diagnosis when an autopsy was performed on me, because I probably would not make it another seventy-two hours.

Tom refused to let his faith stand in the wisdom of man; instead he was determined to stand strong on the power of God, knowing that God would heal me.

I knew that the enemy was trying to take my life and that I was entering into the darkest battle I had ever faced. My family members were called in, and I shared my last wishes with each one of them. My son, Shawn, who had just turned fourteen years old, took my hand and said, "Mom, God is going to heal you because He has given you a promise that has yet to be fulfilled."

For the previous seven years, we had desired to have another child, and on three different occasions through three different prophets, I had received a word from God stating I would conceive and give birth to a male child. God used my son, Shawn, to stir my hope and ignite my faith for this promise that had been confirmed by the prophets, having yet to be fulfilled.

By the next day, I was comatose, suffering severe brain seizures and placed on the terminally ill ward where death was ever present. On many occasions, my monitors would go off and the doctors would rush in and resuscitate me. My husband, sister and mother-in-law sacrificed their lifestyle for me. One of them was at my bedside at all times; 24-7 they played tapes of healing scriptures and God's Word continually in my room. At noon every day, no matter what my son was doing, he would stop and go before God on his knees and pray for his mother's healing.

After six weeks in the Winter Park Hospital, I was transferred by ambulance to Shands Hospital in Gainesville, Florida. After three weeks there, following many tests and procedures, the doctors told Tom he should place me in a nursing facility for my remaining days. Instead, Tom opted to take me home. I weighed less than eighty pounds, and like a baby, I could not walk, talk or do anything for myself. My family took on the responsibility of caring for my every need. Through much prayer, love, therapy and time, I learned how to walk and regained my physical strength, although my mental state had a long way to go.

I was in a very dark and confused place. I had severe hallucinations and had to be restrained often so that I would not injure myself or anyone else. Tom decided to contact Oral Robert's City of Faith Hospital, and they agreed to accept me. After three weeks of being there, Tom came to Tulsa, Oklahoma to bring me home.

God had performed a great work on me. I was no longer violent, and mentally I was much better, except for the fact that I experienced short-term memory loss. The doctors told Tom that because of all the seizures I had suffered, that part of my brain would most likely be permanently damaged. Tom's comment was that God didn't bring us that far to leave us and that He would complete the work He had begun!

God did complete my healing. From the start of this battle until the end took about two years. I went back to Shands Hospital to show the doctors what God had done. All of my brain scans, MRIs and tests were normal! The doctor said to Tom, "You are a mighty man of faith."

Tom's reply was, "I am just an ordinary man with faith in a mighty God!" The doctor agreed that it was a miracle. God had only just begun! On May 24, 1994, exactly seven years from the beginning of my battle, I entered Winter Park Hospital again—only this time instead of facing death, I was giving birth to our son Ceth (Promised of God). As Hebrews 10:23 states, "He who promised is faithful"!

—Victoria McGill

Pearl of Hope

"The kingdom of heaven is like a merchant seeking fine pearls, and upon finding one pearl of great value, he went and sold all that he had and bought it." —Matthew 13:45-46

IMAGINE MY SURPRISE WALKING THE TRAIL AT RICKETT'S Glen State Park in Pennsylvania in May and finding a pearl in the dirt! My sister and I were both surprised when we discovered the word *Hope* engraved on this pearl. I felt hope surge in my heart and still do!

We were there at the park in celebration with family members for my dad, who went home to be with the Lord the previous October. My dad often took us to the park, and we knew it well. So this was a "last hurrah" for us and for him. Our gathering together this time in May was for us to find closure after his burial, as the ground had been frozen in October.

As I examined this pearl, I listened to my heart to see if there was some message from above. Hope came shouting into the picture of our gathering, and as we passed the pearl around, we all felt that, even though Dad was gone, we as a family had hope to carry on in his remembrance. We still find hope as we are continuing to learn from the principles he raised us with.

And if that weren't enough, it was only because of Dad's departure that another family was brought into ours. Little did we know at the time that there was new hope in the heart of a forty-two-year-old gentleman in Ottawa, Canada. While searching for his birth mother on the Internet, our Dad's obituary popped up. His mother turned out to be one of my sisters. He found her because of the obituary! Now that's a whole other story!

Is the pearl real? It probably is not. Is hope real? Absolutely!

—*Andreae Browning*

Hope Realized

"Hope deferred makes the heart sick, but desire fulfilled is a tree of life." —Proverbs 13:12

MY HUSBAND AND I WERE MARRIED IN AUGUST OF 1990. We didn't want to start a family right away as we were getting ready to start college and were fairly young. A week after getting married, we left our tiny island in the Caribbean to attend college. My husband attended Oral Roberts University and I attended Victory Bible Institute in Tulsa, Oklahoma. Five years after graduating college, we returned home to new employment and to work as youth pastors in our local church.

In February of 1995, we were pleasantly surprised with our first pregnancy. However, our joy was short-lived, and nothing prepared us for what happened next. Nineteen weeks into the pregnancy, I unexpectedly went into premature labor and unfortunately lost the baby. Without much explanation as to why this happened, we decided to find comfort in God's Word, while still holding onto our faith.

A few months later, we were expecting again. However, twenty-one weeks into the pregnancy, we went through yet another experience of premature labor and lost our second baby. At this point, we felt hopeless and helpless, especially because at the time, the doctors attending us had no medical explanation as to why this was happening.

We decided to hold off on the idea of trying to get pregnant and start a family for awhile. It took approximately four years before we decided to get pregnant again. This was our third time. By this time, my OB-GYN was able to find out that my cervix was too short. When I would get to a certain point in the pregnancy, my cervix would start to dilate thereby causing premature labor.

In order to try to carry the baby to full term, at fourteen weeks of gestation, I went through a surgical procedure known as cerclage, around the cervix. Unfortunately, this didn't help carry the baby to full term as the doctors intended, and we experienced yet another loss at twenty-four weeks of gestation.

Seven years after our third loss in January of 2007, we were expecting again. This time proactively at fourteen weeks of the pregnancy, we went through the same cerclage procedure again, and I was ordered on bed rest by my OB-GYN, which I strictly adhered to as well. At twenty-four weeks into this fourth pregnancy, I started to go into labor. I went to the emergency room and was early enough to receive medication to stop me from going into premature labor. Only two weeks after the E.R. visit, and still on strict bed rest, I started going into labor again. We immediately rushed back to the hospital. However, this time they were unable to stop the labor. We braced for the worst but were hoping for the best.

On June 3rd, Shekinah Michelle Grace was born, weighing only one pound and fourteen ounces. We were told that being so extremely premature and underweight, she only had a 50 percent chance to pull through, and if she did make it, she would have at least one and probably more complications and disabilities. They said, "She will probably have trouble talking, walking and/or will have to wear glasses at a very young age." Once again, we did what we knew to do best, which was to hold onto God's promises and our faith.

Shekinah had to stay in the NICU for two months, and to the amazement of the doctors and the nurses, she never got sick during her stay, which is usually something that can easily happen to preemies. She did, however, go through the preemies' rollercoaster as far as forgetting to breathe and experiencing heart-rate drops, etc.. But mainly she stayed in the NICU those two months in order to gain weight—which she did!

Shekinah just turned five three weeks ago and is as healthy as a cucumber. She is like the energizer bunny. She keeps going and going and going! She is such a joy and blessing to our lives.

My husband and I were two months shy of our seventeenth wedding anniversary when Shekinah came into our lives. It was most definitely God's Word, our faith in Him and stories similar to this one that gave us hope and encouragement not to give up.

God is good! He is never too late and never too early. There is a time for everything and a season for every activity under heaven! (See Ecclesiastes 3:1 NLT.)

—Lisette Henriette

Hope for the Captive

"Shake yourself from the dust, rise up, O captive Jerusalem; loose yourself from the chains around your neck, O captive daughter of Zion. For thus says the Lord, 'You were sold for nothing and you will be redeemed without money.'" —Isaiah 52:2-3

IT WAS MY NINTH-GRADE YEAR, AND I WAS SITTING IN ALGEBRA class when a tall figure darkened the doorway. It was a police officer, and not to my surprise, he was looking for me. Pretending to be "hard," I rose from my chair with a small smirk on my face. I was placed under arrest and was on my way to the Juvenile Detention Facility. I knew the cop who arrested me, so I asked if I could use his phone to call my mother. He agreed, but I couldn't reach her.

At that moment, I realized I had dug a hole for myself that my mom wouldn't be able to get me out of. There I was, a twelve-year-old facing assault and battery charges for beating a peer with an umbrella and fracturing her arm—all in the name of a gang and a set of colors.

Arriving at the facility and going through the dress-down process was so humiliating, and I could remember thinking, "How did I end up here, and how would I get out of it?" My mother came to the facility expecting to take me home, but they wouldn't allow her. They brought me in a room to see her. The hurt and disappointment in her eyes broke my heart, and the fear in mine broke hers. As the guard entered the room to take me back, tears filled my mother's eyes and ran down her face. "Don't cry, Momma. I will be OK," is what I said. But I wasn't sure about the last part of that statement at all. I wanted to be strong, but as I turned and walked away, weakness consumed me and tears rushed from my eyes.

The next morning, I stood before the judge with two other peers who were involved in the incident with me. The judge addressed our parents about our behavior, and then he looked at us. He called us forward individually and asked what we had to say for ourselves. Nervous and full of fear, I opened my mouth and began to plead with him to let me go home with my mother. I was convinced that I had learned my lesson, and I was trying to convince him of the same. We took our seats, and he announced his verdict to each of us. After sentencing the others involved to three months lockup in the facility, he called my name, and I knew it was over for me. To my surprise, he ordered me to do twenty-eight hours of community service and six months of probation. I was warned that if I got in any trouble within the next six months, I would spend six months in the facility. I was overjoyed! I thought I could go home and put this behind me; but it wasn't over yet.

On Monday, I returned to school, but within the first thirty minutes of homeroom, I was called to the office and expelled for the same reason I was arrested. No! This was not part of my plan! I wanted to finish school, and being out for a year was too big of a problem. My mother came to get me and enrolled me in school in another district. I thought I had beaten the system, but after two weeks, they found me and told me that I wasn't allowed to attend any public school in the city. In rescue mode, my mother enrolled me into a small private school. At first, I hated the school. I didn't like the students or the teachers; I didn't like the principal, and for a long time, I thought she didn't like me. I would skip school to avoid going to this place, and instead of helping my situation, I was making it worse.

At this point, I was very angry and bitter with everyone around me. But they weren't my problem. I was. The problem was I didn't love myself. I saw myself as a failure. I had let everyone down, and I had turned my back on the God I had been taught about all my life. I was so young and had more problems than the average adult. I had spent the last two years of my life indulging in alcohol, drugs and sex. I had even joined a gang. I didn't see a way out of my mess. The hole was too big and too deep, and instead of crawling out, I was being buried under the weight of all the things that I had allowed to consume me. Although my mother was doing everything to fight for me, I didn't have an ounce of strength to fight for myself. I was tired of being a failure, and I was tired of running from my mistakes.

One day while we were having a prayer service in school, the principal called me to come forth, and God spoke to me through her. She said that God knew I was tired of the place where I was and that He was calling me higher. She told me that God was bigger than my problems and that nothing I had ever done would stop Him from loving me. In that prayer service, I felt God embrace me, and I embraced Him back. I wept before God, and my healing process started.

God transformed some things in me that day in a *big* way. I can truly say that my life hasn't been the same since. Within that very year, I pulled my grades up, stopped doing drugs and alcohol, and made a vow to God that I would save myself for marriage. I left school at the end of the year a different person in more ways than one. Although I could've returned to public school the following year, I believed that God wanted me to stay where I was. I talked to my mother, and she agreed.

I learned that everything I needed was in God and that He placed His everything in me. I went on to graduate high school as valedictorian of my class, and I was accepted into a great university on a four-year academic scholarship. God gave me the strength to keep the promises that I made to Him, and He has fulfilled all the promises He made to me. He has protected me from the gang that I thought I could never break free from, and He has given me a husband whom I believe is the very best. God chose me in the midst of brokenness, and in my hopeless situation, I became the epitome of hope!

—Shayla Goldsmith-Tate

Hope for Our Children

"...We also exult in our tribulations, knowing that tribulation brings about perseverance; and perseverance, proven character; and proven character, hope; and hope does not disappoint, because the love of God has been poured out within our hearts through the Holy Spirit who was given to us."
—Romans 5:3-5

GOD HAS INCREDIBLY ENRICHED MY LIFE AND BLESSED ME with four wonderful children: Valerie, Francis Jr., Nina and Olivia. Olivia, who is now seventeen years old, is truly a miracle child. She has had to face several challenges; it took everything I had to believe for a turnaround in each situation.

It all started on October 9, 1994 on what seemed to be a beautiful autumn morning in Plymouth, Minnesota. Not long into the morning, I went into labor. This being my fourth pregnancy, I was sure it would be a breeze. That was the farthest thing from the truth, as I not only had over fourteen hours of labor, but there was no sign of progress. My regular doctor was nowhere to be found, and I was now in the hands of the resident doctors who were not sure what was going on with me.

Since I could no longer take the pain, I asked to be induced. One of the resident doctors showed up to do their routine check on me and the next thing I heard was, "Prepare for an emergency C-section. We need to save this baby now!"

I was immediately wheeled into surgery. Olivia had been bridged for a while and was in distress. Everything happened so quickly and before I knew it, they were putting me under. The surgery started, but the anesthesia did not take. I awakened during surgery, screaming in excruciating pain because I could feel every cut. I could not be given any more anesthetics because I had already received the highest dose. So the doctors administered local anesthetics and advised me to live with the pain.

In a few minutes, Olivia was born and immediately taken away from my sight. Wondering what was going on and too weak to ask, I knew all was not well because I did not hear my baby cry. When I regained consciousness, it was explained to me that Olivia had a few medical problems and would need to stay in the hospital for a while. My heart sank, and I immediately began to pray and remind God of His promises to me. I vacillated between fear and faith for a few minutes, but decided to surround myself with God's Word. I played gospel music and spoke to no one except the Lord.

The doctors came in and told me the details of the problem. Olivia's lungs were not fully developed, and they were collapsing. They feared brain damage and had her on over twenty tubes just to keep her alive. I asked to see her, but I could only see her in the intensive care unit where she was in an incubator. I vacillated between fear and faith. I did not know what to think. I took my little New Testament and went to see tiny Olivia. Tears running down my face, I could see she was fighting for her life. I put my hands over her crib and read Psalm 23 and Psalm 91 and prayed, "Lord, the expectations of the righteous shall not be cut off. I expect Olivia to live and be normal just like You did for my other three. I refuse to see her this way, and I thank You for healing her now." I wondered where such boldness came from, but when you are facing life and death situations, you have to give it your all!

Two days later all the tubes were taken off, Olivia was breathing on her own, and she suffered no brain damage! The doctors asked us to be cautious with her because she would be slow in learning, and they gave us all these restrictions. I refused to believe them because I had seen God move in her life already, and I knew she had a purpose and a destiny.

My family moved to Orlando, Florida when Olivia was four years old. She made it through elementary school and middle school without any struggles, but then came high school. All hell broke loose. When Olivia was in ninth grade, my husband and I went through a terrible divorce, which tore the entire family unit apart. There was instability, chaos and confusion. Olivia was taken away from me for a while and was commuting between two residences. Things got very difficult, and her academic life suffered, as did other areas in her life. All I knew to do was to pray and believe God because He had seen me through so much already.

Olivia struggled, but made it to the eleventh grade. We then began to face new struggles, and I switched schools for her to give her a fresh start. But that fresh start was short-lived. That year, a fellow student slashed Olivia's face as she was getting off the school bus. She was also receiving threats on her life on a popular media website because she was nominated in one of the state teen pageants. Olivia wanted to give up, and even I wanted to give up at times. But our faith in God kept us going.

When twelfth grade came, the struggles continued. We were facing possible homelessness and on top of that, Olivia continued to struggle with her grades. She got to a point where she wanted to give up because she never felt like she would graduate. Her GPA was 1.4 and she failed the FCAT three times. In the midst of that, a broken wall mirror fell on Olivia's leg and cut her four layers deep. She had to have stitches. It was a critical time for her in school, and she could not afford to miss any days. We received notice that Olivia had two days to prove residency or be kicked out of school. I told her that we had to put our trust in God and He would see us through. She registered to take the ACT in lieu of the FCAT, but she failed that three times. On the fourth try, she only passed the math portion of the test. The school counselors told us there was no hope for her to ever graduate.

When it seemed like there was no way out, something rose up inside Olivia and her fighting spirit came back. We marched into the counselor's office who had told us that she would never graduate and told him that she would indeed graduate and nothing could stop her because we had God on our side. The superintendent made an exception for Olivia, and she was able to stay in school.

Olivia was given the opportunity to take the FCAT for the last time a few weeks before her graduation. When her results came back, her counselor said, "Olivia not only passed the FCAT, but she did exceptionally well." She scored one of the highest in the school!

Two days before graduation all of Olivia's grades came in, and she did so well in some of her classes that her grades actually crashed the system. In geometry, which up to that point was one of her worst subjects, she received 104 percent and the progress book online crashed! It was quickly retrieved by the school's staff as they stood in utter amazement at the dramatic turnaround in Olivia's life.

At age seventeen, Olivia walked down the aisle with her diploma on June 2, 2012. Her counselor said, "I never thought it was possible, but you have demonstrated what it means to walk by faith. I am so convinced that all things are possible to those who believe."

God healed Olivia's face without a scar and healed her leg as well. A performing arts college on the West Coast gave Olivia a VIP invitation to attend there and major in dance. The national pageant gave Olivia an open invitation to participate whenever she is ready. Everything the enemy threw at Olivia, God has begun to restore in spite of the challenges we faced. Olivia's faith is stronger than ever and she wants to share her story with other teenagers and young adults on never giving up on their dreams! To God be the glory! Our hope is in Him alone!

—Chidi Jewel Kalu

The Hand of Hope

"For He will give His angels charge concerning you, to guard you in all your ways. They will bear you up in their hands, lest you strike your foot against a stone."
—Psalms 91:11-12

WHEN I WAS AROUND THE AGE OF THIRTEEN, I DECIDED to go to a friend's house for a Bible study. He had the meeting in his backyard by the pool. Moments after the service was finished, I began to converse with his sister. We began to horseplay, and she began chasing me around the swimming pool. For some reason, I felt that I would be able to jump far enough from the side of the deep end to the shallow area of the pool.

To my surprise, my thought was inaccurate, causing me to land in six feet of water. At the time, I was unable to swim and the water began to pull me under. I started to panic, trying desperately to get oxygen. Just as I felt I could no longer hold my breath, I felt a force that lifted me from under the water and landed me safely onto the side of the pool. I looked around to see if someone had jumped in to rescue me, but no one had because they all thought I was just horsing around. I then realized that it was the hand of God that saved my life!

—Andre Tate

Hope for the Hopeless

*Hear, O Lord, and be gracious to me; O Lord, be my helper.' You
have turned for me my mourning into dancing; You have loosed
my sackcloth and girded me with gladness; that my soul may
sing praise to You, and not be silent. O Lord my God, I will give
thanks to You forever." —Psalms 30:10-12*

WHEN I CAME TO ORLANDO, I CAME WITH A LOT OF BAGGAGE,
and it didn't begin with my move. It started from childhood.

As a little girl of five years old, I remember being molested
by my two cousins. That led to feelings of being less than a fe-
male. I felt like I was not loved because if I was, how could this
be happening to me? I was afraid to tell anyone because I was
afraid I would be blamed and told that I was the one responsible for this happening to me. I silently carried my pain, and
when things would go wrong in my life, I would tell myself that
I was deserving of it and had brought it upon myself.

Each time the abuse occurred, the feelings of being unloved
grew. I felt less than a person, and I never felt like I was a woman.

Even as I got into adulthood, these feelings stripped me of
everything I thought a woman should be. I felt as though I were
unworthy of love; especially the love of a man. As the years
went on the thoughts of being unloved, rejected and contami-
nated were ever present. This led to feelings of depression.

I became discouraged to the point of feeling hopeless, and
didn't see a way out. Every day was just another day. I existed
because I had nothing else to do and no way out. I didn't know
what joy or happiness really was. Then there were times when
I truly tried to find love in all the wrong places. I experienced
constant fear and suicidal thoughts.

The doctors tried to help, but I became dependent on the
drugs that they prescribed. I felt like my family didn't want me
around, and I wondered if I was adopted. The more I tried to get

their love and acceptance, the more I was rejected. It became a vicious cycle. I wondered, "Does anybody love me? Can anybody ever love me? Am I even worthy of love?"

In the lowest season of my life, not only was I experiencing brokenness, but I became homeless and was living out of my car and sleeping in the church parking lot. I would not let anyone know of my plight because of my pride. I was working part time and began giving 10 percent of my income to the church I was attending. During this time, I rededicated my life to Christ and began believing that there might be a way out of my circumstances.

I began to learn about healing and forgiveness. I went and sought counseling from my church. I stopped taking the drugs that I was on. I began to accept that I was not the person that my family had made me become. I was truly loved by God in spite of what had taken place. I may have been a victim when I was a young girl, but I began to realize that I had control of my feelings now as an adult. The more I read the Word, the more I began to change.

I began to tell myself in the morning that I was free to love myself. No matter what I saw reflected in the mirror as I got ready, I was free to love myself. I began to see that I was not broken and I was not in despair. I had hope because I realized that the Word was true and God loved me! God made me in His image, and I was beautiful to Him!

I stand in awe over what God has done in my life. After ninety days of being homeless, He gave me an apartment that was brand-new. I went back to school and earned my degree—not one degree, but I earned two degrees. I have an Associate of Arts in Bible and a Bachelor of Science in Christian Leadership and Ministry. I have even been blessed to own my own home!

When I look at life now, I see it through new lenses. To sum up my life, I would have to say that there is one word that really stands out for me and that word is *love!*

—*Ruth Cooper*

Hope for an Open Door

"And as you go, preach, saying, 'The kingdom of heaven is at hand.' Heal the sick, raise the dead, cleanse the lepers, cast out demons. Freely you received, freely give." —Matthew 10:7-8

IN THE LATTER PART OF 1994, I KNEW THAT GOD WAS GOING to send me on another mission trip. This would be the sixth trip that I would be blessed to be a part of, and of them all it would prove to be the greatest experience of the faithfulness and provision of God. I had been praying to go to India, so I began a series of shots for this possible adventure. The door to India never opened, so I began to receive shots required to go to Africa. I was still unaware, however, where or when my next trip would actually be.

During a partners' conference I was attending, it was announced that a team would be going to Zambia, Africa and there were fourteen openings left. I knew in my heart that I was to go on this trip. The cost was announced to be $3,393, and I knew I didn't have a dime. I had to trust God for the finances and felt His leading not to send out any letters for support but to fully trust Him for the necessary finances. I told the Lord that if He provided the finances, I would be obedient to go.

I proceeded to apply for two loans to try and finance my trip to Africa only to be turned down. After about two weeks, I finally got my first financial breakthrough. I received $2,000. A friend asked me, "If God is sending you to Africa, don't you think He will give you all of the money, and not just part of it?" I replied that I had asked myself the same question, but I was going to proceed in faith.

I called the church and spoke with Ruth, the tour coordinator. I told her that I had just received $2,000 and was trusting God for the rest.

I later found out that the $3,393 only included the price from New York to Africa. I was faced with another problem. In addition to the $3,393 (which I still did not have in full) I needed the cost of a round-trip ticket to New York to make the connecting flight. I found this out on Wednesday afternoon, and the flight for Zambia was scheduled on Friday. I had hoped to purchase a buddy pass for $150 from my sister who works for Continental Airlines. She informed me that I would not be able to get a pass from her. I called Delta Airlines and discovered that the cost of a round trip ticket to JFK would be $516. I hung up from Delta and was on hold with U.S. Air, when I responded to my phone's call-waiting signal. The voice on the other end of the line asked if I was Marva. I answered, "Yes," and she indicated that a round-trip ticket to New York had been sown into my life. I hung up the phone and had a praise celebration with my son! I now had $2,000 and an airline ticket to New York; but I still needed $1,393 for the balance of my trip.

I was so excited that I called Ruth and left a message that I had just received a round-trip ticket to New York and was trusting God for the remaining finances for my trip. She later returned my call and asked if I had my passport and visa. I was unaware of the fact that I needed a visa for this trip. She indicated the only way I could possibly get a visa in one day was to drive down to Miami. The next morning, I got up around 5 A.M. and headed off to Miami, only to discover once I arrived that I would not be able to get a visa to Zambia there. I called Ruth and informed her of these events. She indicated her regret and told me to return home, and I could only trust God to get a visa once I arrived in Zambia. If I could not get a visa in Zambia, I would have to turn around and fly home. I didn't complain and continued to believe God that I would be going to Zambia. Ruth shared with me that she had previously worked for *The 700 Club* before coming to Orlando, and over the years she had heard several thousand people tell her that by faith they were believing God to go on a mission trip; but this was the first time she had actually witnessed someone walk out their faith and trust God to make a way out of no way. I began to pray earnestly that God would provide a way for me to make this trip.

Well it was now Thursday afternoon and the plane was leaving Friday morning and I still needed $1,393 and my visa. By faith, I went to the credit union and got $300 in traveler's checks. I then went to the Orange County Health Department to make sure I had all the necessary shots to enter Zambia. I know it was the favor of God that I was able to walk right in and be waited on because I did not have an appointment. My file was up to date and I didn't need to pay anything to receive more shots. If I had not believed God in 1994, I never would have had the necessary shots for this trip.

I was down to the last two hours before I needed to board my flight to New York. I called Betty who had been praying and agreeing with me for God's provision all along the way. I asked her if I should give up or pack my clothes by faith since I still needed the $1,393 to complete the cost of my trip. At around 5 P.M., I received a call from Ruth. She asked me if I was packed and ready to go. I responded that I had a few things packed and she told me I was going. The balance of the money had just been paid! My phone rang again and it was Betty from choir. She indicated my ticket was being ordered from Mighty Eagle. God had been speaking to Betty all day to make a certain phone call and she obeyed. Truly God is faithful to His promise!

I now had all my finances for the trip but still had to trust God for my visa. When we landed in Johannesburg, South Africa, the lady looked at my passport and told me I was going to have a big problem when I got to Zambia. I just whispered a silent prayer and continued to keep my eyes on the promise of God's faithfulness.

As we approached Zambia, Ruth said, "Marva, this is it! Start praying in the Spirit." Pastor Fred looked at me and said, "You are truly a lady full of faith." As the plane landed, a beautiful awareness of the love of God embraced me and I began to cry. I knew then that God had not brought me on this journey of faith in vain and He had already supplied my every need; therefore, He would allow me to go into this country.

Ruth had faxed the government ahead of our arrival explaining the situation, and when we landed, there was a gentleman from the president's cabinet waiting to greet us. He had received the fax, and he was sent to help me obtain my visa. Some of the members of the team looked at me in shock. Yes, God is faithful, but the question is, how far are you willing to trust Him and the promises that He has given?

—Marva

The Hope of a Child

At the same time came the disciples unto Jesus, saying, Who
is the greatest in the kingdom of heaven? And Jesus called a
little child unto him, and set him in the midst of them, and said,
Verily, I say unto you, except ye be converted, and become as
little children, ye shall not enter into the kingdom of heaven.
Whosoever therefore shall humble himself as this little child,
the same is greatest in the kingdom of heaven."
—Matthew 18:1-4 (KJV)

I REMEMBER AS A CHILD ALWAYS HAVING A LOVE FOR ANIMALS. Every book I read was on wildlife of some kind. I remember desperately wanting a dog of my own, but my father was allergic to them; therefore I was not permitted to have one. I told him simply with my childlike faith that I would pray that God would heal him of his allergies and then we could get a dog.

Never question the faith of a child because, sure enough, my father received his healing and we got a dog. She was a little white poodle that we named Peaches because she had a hint of apricot in her coat. I loved my little dog and she quickly became a part of our family.

My father was a hardworking man and my mom stayed home to raise us children. We would have been considered upper middle class. We were comfortable, but with four children to provide for, money was tight at times.

One day we were playing with Peaches and as she was running after us down the stairs, she lost her footing and fell all the way down the stairs. When she reached the bottom, we soon discovered that she had injured her back and was in terrible pain. I ran to my father and told him what had happened and declared that we needed to hurry and bring her to the vet. My dad responded that we did not have the money to afford the vet bill. Well I knew that if God had healed my dad so we could get this little dog, He could just as easily heal her of this back injury. So we all got around Peaches and laid hands on her and asked the Lord to heal her. She instantly stopped whining and got up and started to run around! She was totally healed! Never underestimate the faith of a child!

—Anonymous

Hope in the Midst of Darkness

"And Jesus said to him, '...All things are possible to him who believes.'" —Mark 9:23

All Hell Breaks Loose

A LONG TIME AGO, I WAS TOLD BY SEVERAL DOCTORS THAT conceiving a child would be next to impossible because I did not have all the "inner workings" necessary to help make that happen. I accepted this prognosis and went on with my life. In 2005, on the night of my honeymoon, we conceived our first son, Gavin. My husband and I were both stunned and so was the doctor. I was pretty excited and nervous all at the same time. I had my first appointment with the doctor when I was four months along, and on that day, two things were brought to light. First I was informed that I had severe dysplasia; second I was told that my husband was a confirmed heroin addict.

My faith seemed smaller than a mustard seed and at the time, all my spiritual education came from the Bible. The pastor was teaching and preaching on God's goodness. About two weeks later (I recall it was a Wednesday), the biopsy results came in. This was the day that I had to drop my husband off at a Christian rehab center as an inpatient for nine months. After saying our extremely emotional good-byes and praying that God would give me strength for the day, I went on my way to the doctor's appointment.

As I laid on the table waiting for the results, a nurse walked in and asked if my husband was with me. I, of course, told her no while thinking to myself, "If only you knew I just dropped him off at a rehab center, and I am not going to be able to see him for six weeks!" After six weeks, I would be able to see him one to two times per week, and that was only at church services. She breathed a deep sigh, and in came the doctor. She looked at me and said, "Mrs. Westenskow, you have an aggressive form of cervical cancer that is going to require chemotherapy immediately."

I must have been staring into space for quite some time because I heard my name called several times before I was able to respond. After I snapped out of it, my response was, "I do not believe that God would open my womb and bless me with the ability to carry a child after being told I could not, and not let me carry, deliver and raise this child."

She replied, "Mrs. Westenskow, the chance of your survival is very slim without treatment. The treatment will cause harm to the fetus, and if we do not treat it right away, you risk your life and the fetus." I left the office that afternoon feeling numb. Is this really my life? Was I really pregnant and married to a heroin addict? Do I really have cancer right now? What???!!! I sat in my car and began to weep uncontrollably. I felt like a failure in life. Did I mention that I also had to give up my apartment and move in with my in-laws? No husband, no job, no home—oh yeah—and cancer!

After what seemed like the longest day of my life, I began to go through some of my notes from church. I read things like God is a miracle-working God and God is a good God all the time. I shared the news with my mother-in-law, and she said something that to this day I have never forgotten. She said, "Natalie, God is whatever you need Him to be at the time that you need Him to be it." Those words fell over me like a warm blanket on an extremely cold evening. My response to her at the time was, "Mom, I cannot bring myself to believe that God would open up my womb and bless me with the opportunity to have a child and not let me raise him."

Month after month, I was told by doctors to abort and try conceiving again when my health was better. Each time I said no. David, my husband, had no clue what I was going through because I did not want anything to distract him from getting better. I thanked God every night for the child growing inside me. When I felt lonely, I invited the Holy Spirit to keep me company. I fought back thoughts of, "You're crazy talking to yourself like that! You're acting like a fool! You're alone and you're always going to be alone!" Dr. Mark Chironna once said, "The devil will kick you while you're down."

Still, I hung on to hope. Hope in Christ! Hope in His Word that says He is a good God all the time! Hope in Luke 18:27: *"Jesus replied, 'What is impossible with men is possible with God'"* (NIV). The doctors could not help me so God had to! I would like to share with you Dr. Mark Chironna's definition of grace: "I can't, so He has to."

I Can See the Light

The following is my journal entry on a Tuesday morning in January, 2006:

Trinity:

As I lay here in my bed, unable to see past my belly, I cannot seem to shake the feeling that something wonderful is about to happen. Maybe that something will be at church tonight? One more month until I am able to hold Gavin in my arms! I am so excited! I cannot believe what this year has been like. I know I could not have done it without You, Lord. Thank You.

—NRW

On the Friday evening following the journal entry, I visited David. The ministry that was assisting him with his addiction was having an evening service, and I really missed my husband. When I arrived, I found him waiting in the pew with two new Bibles in his hands. He greeted me with the best hug and belly rub. He kissed me on my forehead, cheeks, lips and, of course, the belly. He was so happy to see me and expressed it freely and openly, which is something he rarely did. Everything in me screamed, "This is it! This is the something wonderful!" I was convinced nothing could top this! That is until praise and worship started.

It took just a few minutes for me to feel comfortable closing my eyes and worshipping alongside my husband. I kept looking around the room, taking in every face. Suddenly a light began to shine by David's feet, and when I looked up, I saw the most incredible thing: I saw a light shining on my husband! It looked as though it may have been coming from inside him! How? I put my hands to my mouth in awe of what I was seeing. *Deliverance!*

"Dear God!" I cried out, "Thank You!" as I fell to my knees in worship. I cried uncontrollably for what seemed like an hour. I went home that night thanking God. When I walked through the door, I could not contain the excitement, and shared my experience with my mother-in-law.

Here is another journal entry, from February 10, 2006:

The Birth:

I am about ten days away from my due date. I am so excited! My mom and David's mom surprised me with a painted nursery with all the colors I wanted. They love me and I love them. I went to see the doctor for my weekly checkup. At first, I was scared that they were going to harass me again, but that's not what I experienced this time. This doctor was different. He said he was a Christian; said he did not get many opportunities to share his love of Christ with his patients. My guard was up! I was ready to attack him if he so much as suggested I abort! Instead what he said left me stunned: "Mrs. Westenskow, I have been studying your file, and I believe we can deliver Gavin safely and with His help, remove most of the cancer. If this works, all we will need to do after the delivery is a leap procedure that will remove the majority, if not all, of your cervix."

I asked, "Has this been done before?" to which he replies, "No." Great! Talk about walking in faith! "When you go to deliver, we will need for you to sit at a 45-degree angle which will put more pressure on the baby and cause a squeezing that will help him move through the canal quicker. The squeezing will cause the baby to press against the cervix, bruising it severely and causing some of the mass, if not all, to come out with him."

—NRW

At 10 P.M. on a Friday night, I was standing in line waiting to be prayed for concerning generational curses. As the pastor laid his hands on me I instantly went down to the floor. As I lay there, I heard a still, small voice internally say, "It's time." I knew it meant Gavin was coming. I requested to be helped up and very slowly walked over to my husband and whispered in his ear, "It's time." He responded with a swift, speedy rush out the front door of the church. All was wonderful, except for the fact that he left without me! Four men came to my aide and began to bicker amongst themselves as to who would carry me out. All the while I kept on trying to move forward but got held back until a decision was made! It's a good thing God is patient. By the time a decision was made, Dave was back inside and commanded them to release me so that he could get me to the car. My hero!

After a delicious meal, we arrived at the hospital and within minutes, I was admitted into a delivery room. About an hour later, I was settled in my bed and the doctor walked in and stated that Gavin should arrive around 7 A.M., which was three hours out. After about twenty minutes, I opened my eyes and saw this thick cloud hovering above me. It looked as if it was taking over the ceiling! I closed my eyes and opened them again, and it was still there. I also began to think I was a bit high on drugs, except that drugs were given to me between ten and fifteen minutes *after* my experience. I asked David if he was seeing what I was seeing, and he said no. However, he could feel the Holy Spirit present in the room. Wow! My first Holy Spirit encounter! Awesome! Shortly after, the midwife came to my side and said I was delivering a very special child. Her voice was soft and loving and comforting to hear.

At 5:10 A.M. and without any pain or contractions, Gavin was born and—would you believe it—he tore through the mass causing most of it to come out with him. A miracle! A womb transformed from barrenness to fruitfulness!

Glory to God! Shortly after Gavin was born, a leap procedure was done to remove what was left of the cancerous mass. Not only did God say, "Yes" when doctors said, "No," but God gave me the hope I needed in His Word to help get me through.

"What is impossible with man is possible with God."

—Natalie Westenskow

Hope for a New Life

"The thief cometh not, but for to steal, and to kill, and to destroy; I am come that they might have life, and that they might have it more abundantly." —John 10:10 (KJV)

FOR MANY YEARS, I HAVE LIVED A HAPPY, FULFILLING LIFE, but that was not always so. A dark hopelessness had enveloped my life from the time I was a child. Dysfunctional family? That was an understatement! There were years of violence, drunken arguments and broken glass. The police had been called to our house a few times. My mother wore sunglasses many times to conceal bruises she had sustained from the most recent fight. I watched helplessly as she married what seemed to be the same man over and over again. Men who were a lot of fun and enjoyed music and drink, but would eventually have fits of anger.

I would often go outside, amidst the shouts ringing from my house and look up at the stars and wonder if things would ever change. I would think, "Where is God?" And yet, looking up at the stars, for a moment, I didn't feel totally alone.

The atmosphere in our home seemed to become more and more angry. In fact, my mother in particular seemed especially hostile to me at times. I couldn't understand her sudden mood swings toward me. It wasn't until years later that I learned she had been raped as a young woman. She was married at the time, and when she became pregnant, she wasn't sure if I was the result of that rape or not. Although my mother had been through a lot and dealt with a lot of emotional pain, she really tried to do the best she could to take care of my older brother and me. I repressed my own confusion and anger by reading everything I could find, watching old movies, sketching and learning all I could about horses and being a teenager.

A big change came in 1970 when our house burnt down from an electrical fire. The rest of my family was out of town at the time. At one o'clock in the morning, I stood shivering in a cold March wind watching the flames eat away at our old style Florida home. I thought so many things..."How am I going to tell my mother her house burnt down? Everything is going to change. It's over! Life will never be the same. It's got to be better!"

Later that morning, my mother returned to find the house in a heap of ashes. Shortly after that event, I moved up the west coast of Florida to live with my brother and his family. My mother stayed in South Florida and eventually moved to Denver.

For almost ten years I used drugs as a kind of anesthesia to dull the pain I felt. The dark heaviness I had felt throughout my childhood only got heavier. I gradually got an apartment of my own and began waitressing to pay the bills. Despite constantly being high, I managed to work. My mother had drummed a few basic principles into me, and having a strong work ethic was one of them. Another was that you respected God. There was only one God, she would say, and He deserved respect. That one principle eventually would be a life-changing key for me. Outside of that, I knew very little about God. We didn't attend church as a family. If I behaved poorly, my frustrated mother would send me a couple of blocks away to a small church. I would sit in the back and draw on the bulletins while I would observe all the "old people." Wow, I remember thinking, I guess church is just for old people, and for many years, I didn't give God or church another thought.

My apartment was near the beach and, almost daily, I would go and sit on the beach and ponder my life. I found a small amount of comfort in the beauty of the sky and the gentle ebb and flow of the tide. The people who passed by me laughed and played along the shore with such a freedom I knew I didn't have. "My life is over," I would think. "But I'm so young, how could it be over?" I often thought maybe I could just kill myself. I was so tormented! I would dread the morning, and when the morning came, I couldn't wait for it to be night. Later I would read a similar scripture in the Book of Psalms.

One day I experienced a true miracle. My boyfriend and I, along with another couple, decided to go to a rock concert in Tampa. Against our better judgment, we decided to drink some mushroom tea on the way, which is a strong hallucinogenic. The plan was originally to sip the tea just before going into the concert. But about halfway between Sarasota and Tampa, we stopped at a convenience store and got some Dixie cups and soda to drink with the tea. We started driving again and in minutes, the world around us melted into a liquid maze of vibrant color. Everything seemed to be moving in slow motion. The median strips looked like they were splashing against the car.

At one point, my overwhelmed boyfriend made a wrong turn and headed us into oncoming traffic! Somehow, he managed to get the car turned around and headed back in the right direction of traffic. Suddenly, I knew we had to park the car as soon as possible...but where? Almost instantly, I looked to my right and saw a sign that said *Parking*. It was so big it seemed to be written in the sky! I said to my boyfriend, "Why don't we park there?" With a big sigh of relief he said, "OK," and pulled into a parking garage. We sat in the car a few minutes to pull ourselves together after our wild ride. Although we were still a little high, most of the hallucinating had stopped. As soon as we got out of the car I noticed a lot of young people walking hurriedly to a building across the street. I said out loud as we passed the parking garage attendant, "I wonder if these people are going to the concert?"

Hearing me, the attendant answered, "Yes, that's where they're going." I was amazed as I thought he couldn't possibly know what I was talking about. But he was right. We had stopped at the parking garage adjacent to the concert! I was absolutely shocked! We really didn't have a clue how we got there! We didn't get us there! God got us there! He not only got us there, He protected us and everyone else from us!

I sat through the entire concert reeling with the realization that God had intervened! I knew I was never going to do drugs again. God had spared my life and probably many others. At two o'clock in the morning over breakfast, I made my announcement to my friends. "I'm never doing drugs again," I said. No one believed me since they had rarely seen me when I was not high. But I meant it! God had somehow spared my life and I wasn't about to treat it lightly.

Life improved somewhat when I quit doing drugs. I even voted for the first time in a presidential election. It was the first time I knew who was running! I slept better and ate healthier. Still the dark heaviness remained. I decided to take up Transcendental Meditation (TM) and a kind of peace seemed to come into my life. I attributed the slight relief to TM even though a couple of things about TM bothered me. For one, the initiation ceremony puzzled me. I was told to bring a handkerchief and a couple of pieces of fruit and my teacher would then present them while he chanted thanks over a picture of Maharishi Mahesh Yogi on my behalf. I had no idea what it meant. When I asked what significance it held for me, I was told none. My teacher was simply giving thanks to Maharishi for bringing this "great knowledge to light." Daily I became more dedicated to TM as order and some semblance of peace seemed to increase in my life. My goal became to go to India and train to become a TM teacher. But that ended when I had another miracle.

I was at the breakfast table reading over a flyer I had gotten the night before from some Christians who had protested a meeting we were having regarding TM. The flyer accused TM of being a cult and specifically mentioned the initiation ceremony. They had said that the fruit and handkerchief were symbolic of an offering to a false god.

Suddenly the room I was in was filled with a blinding light! I couldn't see anything but scenes of my life flashing before my eyes like a rapid slideshow! At the same time, I heard a voice from deep within me say, "You have had an enemy your whole life and not known it!"

Immediately I knew that voice was talking to me about the devil. I had felt the presence of demons for years when I did drugs. Suddenly, I realized my enemy all along was the devil. He had somehow been behind so many horrible events in my life that had just been shown to me in that slideshow. I said right out loud, "Devil! You are so about nothing! Because if you were about *something,* you wouldn't have to trick people into following you! I'm going to find God, and there's nothing you can do to stop me!"

So, I set out to find God. But I was so confused. None of the friends I talked to seemed to know what I was talking about when I asked them about God. I would tell them I felt like God wanted me to do something, but what? No one seemed to have the answer, and I couldn't go back to the church of old folks! Frustrated, one day I said out loud into the air, "If You are really God, then You are fully capable of revealing Yourself to me! So I am leaving it up to You!" The thread of hope that was within me was getting stronger and stronger!

One day while waitressing, I found a tract on my table. I opened it up and it said, "Do you want to know God?" Wow! I couldn't wait to get home and read it! I stuffed the tract in my pocket and as soon as I got home, I went into my bedroom and shut the door. I pulled out the tract and read that God loved me, died for me, and I needed to ask for forgiveness and receive Jesus into my heart. I stood in the middle of my room, closed my eyes and did exactly what the tract said. Immediately I felt the heaviness lift off of me! It seemed like my own height and body weight changed. I actually seemed to stand up taller!

The heaviness was replaced with something pouring into me that could only be described as cool water. I laughed and cried all night with such joy I had never known. I sang every hymn I could think of! I couldn't wait for daylight! This time I had to tell everyone I knew what God had done for me! Most didn't even wait to hear and would immediately ask, what *happened* to you? The thread of hope that had kept me all those years had become the rope of safety I needed. Not only did my life change forever, but dreams I never knew I had began to emerge. Shortly after that, I found a great church and started a new job selling advertising. My whole life changed and I have never been the same! Thank You, Jesus!

—Rebecca

The Fruit of Hope

"And whatsoever ye shall ask in my name, that will I do, that the Father may be glorified in the Son. If ye shall ask any thing in my name, I will do it." —John 14:13-14 (KJV)

BACK IN THE MID 1980S, MY HUSBAND AND I WERE TRAVELING full time in ministry. We made our living going from meeting to meeting and saw God move in the lives of many people as a result of our ministry. After a few years on the road, my heart longed for a place to call home as all our worldly possessions were in storage, and we traveled only with a few suitcases filled with clothes.

The Lord was good and opened a door for us to go on staff part time at a wonderful church in Pittsburgh. Because the church at that time was small, they could only afford to give us a small salary and we would continue to make the bulk of our income from the road. But we were thrilled to have some place to finally call home and get that sense of rootedness. I remember the pastor told us that this would be a season where we would learn to trust God in a new way for our provision. We were required to be home three Sundays out of the month and would be permitted to travel for meetings during the week and one Sunday a month. Since the majority of our larger meetings were on Sundays, this would cut into our income considerably. We knew God was leading us to this church and agreed to these stipulations.

That began our journey on a path to see God make a way out of no way on many occasions for us in the area of provision. I can remember when it got so tight we would have to purchase our groceries on credit cards because we did not have any money left after paying the rent on our apartment. But the Lord was using our pastor and this church as a tool of healing and refreshing after being on the road so long without anywhere to call home.

I remember one day the pastor calling us into his office and telling us it was time we considered purchasing a home. I knew that we had only one thousand dollars in our savings account and were living honorarium to honorarium, but I also heard the voice of God in his voice and made a decision at that moment to accept this as the will of God and believe that He would work out the seemingly impossible for us.

I began by making a list of everything that I wanted in a house. My husband was the practical one and started with what he felt would be a reasonable amount to pay for a house. He said he felt we could afford a home that cost around $40,000. So I agreed and began writing down what I wanted in my $40,000 home. I wrote down that it had to have three bedrooms, a living room, kitchen and a finished basement. Oh, and it had to have a fenced-in backyard because I wanted to get a dog!

The next thing we did was to get a real estate agent to show us available properties. We told him what we desired and what we felt we could afford, but we didn't tell him that we only had one thousand dollars to our name! He was so kind and took us around and showed us property after property, but nothing matched the list we had created. The properties that we loved were too expensive and the ones in our price range were not what we wanted. I kept holding on to my faith that God was leading us to purchase a home and that the one He had for us was out there.

After a few months of looking and not finding what we wanted, we decided to hold off buying a home. We got discouraged and felt like it might not be the right time. We told our real estate agent that we were done for the moment. A few weeks later, he called us after church on a Sunday and told us we had to meet him and see this new listing. At first we said no, but he persisted. We gave in and met him at the home he wanted to show us. The moment I walked in the door, my spirit leaped within me and I knew this was our house—even before receiving the grand tour! Sure enough, everything that was in this house was on my list. It had three bedrooms, a full kitchen and living room, a finished basement, and it even had a fenced-in backyard! And my husband was thrilled because it was in our $40,000 price range!

The realtor told us to put down a security deposit on the house and then we could proceed with getting everything in order for the purchase. We wrote out a check for one thousand dollars but didn't tell him that was all of our money. We signed the papers for the deposit and when he ran the figures, he told us we would have to come up with $7,000 for the closing, which would take place in thirty days. Well $7,000 might as well have been $7,000,000 to us! But we smiled and told him that we would have it.

We went back and told our pastor what had transpired, and he told us that God would provide everything we needed for the closing. Little did we know, but that would begin a thirty-day process of one of the biggest tests of our faith. We had no one else to rely on but God. I remember we would go from faith to worry in what felt like a roller coaster ride seemingly moment to moment. We prayed about it constantly. I am not so sure whether our reminding God was a stand of faith or a frantic reality that if He didn't provide the $7,000, we would lose the house and our thousand dollars.

I remember at the close of one of our home meetings, we were having a time of prayer and my husband had asked the group to agree with us that God would provide the down payment for our home. While we were praying, I opened my eyes and looked at the sliding glass doors in the living room of our apartment. The doors were closed and it was nighttime. While everyone was praying, the curtain began to blow and a bright white light shone behind the curtain. I knew there was no natural source for the movement of the curtain or the light, and I realized it was God's way of showing me that He would provide everything we needed for the closing and that home would be ours. After the meeting was over and everyone had gone home,

I told my husband what I had seen and the assurance of faith that had entered my spirit. From that moment one, I had no more doubt that God was going to provide.

Well, we came upon the day of the closing and had only one hour left before we had to meet with the realtor to give him the money and sign all the papers. We had not yet received a penny toward our closing! Talk about a test of faith! Either God was going to have to show up or we would look like fools for believing Him! Right before we were to walk out the door from the church to head for the realtor's office, our pastor called us into his office. He told us to sit down and then handed my husband an envelope. He opened it up and wept as he found inside $7,000. Someone had come to our pastor and told him that God had spoken to them to give us this money! We don't know who they were, but have prayed a blessing over them for their generosity and their obedience! Not only did that amount cover all our closing costs, we even had enough money left over to rent a moving truck and move all our belongings into our new home!

God is indeed faithful! Not only did that home prove to be a blessing to us in the natural, but more importantly it taught us to believe God for His provision when it seems like there is absolutely no way for the situation to work out!

—*Ruth Chironna*

Hope for the Broken

"If your heart is broken, you'll find God right there; if you're kicked in the gut, he'll help you catch your breath. Disciples so often get into trouble; still, God is there every time. He's your bodyguard, shielding every bone; not even a finger gets broken."
—Psalms 34:18-20 (The Message)

ONE OF MY GIRLFRIENDS AND I WENT TO CABO SAN LUCAS for a vacation one year. We spent six days and nights having a wonderful time enjoying the scenery, pools, local cuisine and generally having a good time. The entire week, however, my friend, Betty, wanted to swim in the ocean, but we never could because the tide was very rough and the flags were always red, warning all swimmers not to enter.

On the fifth night, we were having dinner on the beach, enjoying the ten-foot tall waves as our backdrop. I mentioned to her how the water seemed to beckon me. I commented that water was a mysterious death, leaving no bodies, no carnage. Death by water was not like being in a car crash or fire, where there were remains. The water took people. It took the Titanic, the Lusitania and many others. Then the waves just kept silently hitting the shore, hiding the souls within it. There was only the sound and sights of the thunderous waves crashing against the shore. It was eerie but beautiful.

The next day, one day before we were to leave, the ocean calmed and the flags were green. We were on the beach and noticed about twelve people bopping in the water. So we got up and walked to the spot in between the green flags where the people were safely floating and enjoying the water. We were about thirty feet from the shore, still on dry land with our sandals on when a huge wave came up on shore and hit our ankles. We were not yet within the green flag zone, but we were on dry land, so we just kept walking, not thinking too much of this. The next wave came up to our mid-calves, but we kept getting closer to the green flags and walked parallel to the shore. The final wave came up to my knees and was about two feet high. As the water pushed to shore, it pulled the sand from under our feet until neither of us could stand. We both fell down, and as the water rushed back into the ocean, it took both of us with it.

I remember being swept into the water and while still sliding out to the depths, being slammed onto a rock, upside down. It felt like it tore off my leg at the knee, and the water held me there for a few seconds. A sharp pain went through my body, and I was helpless as the wave lifted me up and took me out yet further. The pain was unbearable, and I wasn't even aware of what was happening. Soon I found air, and I barely got a gulp of it before more water came crashing down upon me, taking me further and deeper into the ocean. Still, the pain in my leg was predominant over the crashing water. I was tossed this way a couple more times. One time my head came up, and as I looked behind me trying to see when the next wave was coming, I saw the wave right there. I looked up and up, thinking maybe I could bodysurf it, but it was about eight feet tall, and I was too close to its base to get to the top of it. As this particular wave hit, it was exceedingly strong. It took me down and held me in an apex, neither moving up nor down, just stuck underwater. I don't know how deep the water was, but in retrospect, the people on the shore, now gathered and watching, were very tiny. I guess I had been taken and tumbled about 100 yards or so.

As a side note, my brother was a Navy SEAL when he was younger. He learned that I had been swimming to get in bathing-suit shape for Cabo and had challenged me, saying that he used to swim three lengths underwater when he was a SEAL, never coming up for air. Let's see if I could do that! Well, not to be outdone by my brother, I began practicing. Even before my trip, I had increased my stamina about five times and had gone from swimming five strokes to half length without air, and a full width underwater. I now know this friendly competition between my brother and me was the Holy Spirit preparing me for what was to come in Cabo.

As I was still being held in some bizarre spot underwater, I thought I would open my eyes and swim to the top. I was a strong swimmer and was not afraid, but I could not seem to make heads nor tails of which way was up, and my strength was wearing very thin. I didn't have much energy to keep fighting. The pain in my leg had all but been eclipsed by my inability to breathe. I didn't know if I had a leg or not and had a thought about being either hit by a boat or having sharks attack me—because of the imagined blood on my leg. When I opened my eyes, things got worse. There was no top. I had been turned over and upside down and tossed so many times, and I was at such a depth that I could not discern which way was up. The water mixed with sand swirled around me. It was translucent, and I was in a suspension that was neither taking me deeper or higher. The ocean had me in its grasp, and it was holding me, not even releasing me for air this time.

I then had a thought that started in my stomach. That was the first time I ever "felt" a thought. It rose quickly to my brain where it was deciphered. The thought was, "Hold your breath, the water will lift you up." I felt it as sure as if it were a fish swimming up my lungs and into my brain. I had never felt a thought originate from my stomach like that. But I listened to the voice, closed my eyes and continued to hold my breath, and the water did eventually lift me up.

As was now normal routine, once on top and able to breathe, I quickly turned around to see the next wave and its size and anticipate the next horror. But when I turned around to see the waves, the ocean was as calm as an evening sunset. There were no waves, no residuals, nothing. It was over. I no longer felt the pain in my leg. I could see land and started to semi-swim toward it.

I wasn't really "swimming" but kind of pushing forward. I happened to swim up next to my friend, who had not been taken out as far. I had all but forgotten about her. She was treading water, turning in circles. When she faced me, I saw her eyes as big as quarters, and she kept saying, "I don't know which way to swim; I don't know which way to swim."

I said, "Betty, toward the land, toward the land." She didn't hear me, and I was about to touch her arm to get her attention when another thought that started from my stomach "swam" up to my brain. This time the thought said, "Don't touch her." I wanted to fight it, but it came again, "Don't touch her." With nothing else to do, I pointed to the shore and yelled again, "Toward land!" Then I turned around and left her as I swam toward land myself. Looking back, I know that was the Holy Spirit and I praise Him for saving her. I kept swimming and left her—what a friend! It is hard to think about that every time I remember this story—that I just left my friend who was in shock. I left her.

As I got closer to shore, there was a man standing right next to the green flag. There were thirty or so people on the shoreline and only this one man was standing in the water with his hand outstretched. He yelled to me, "Need some help?" At first I didn't understand him or even realize he was talking. He said it again, "Need some help?" and it was like my brain suddenly returned to my body. I saw him, I heard him and yes I needed some help! "Yes! Yes!" I began yelling back at him, for there was still a great distance between us and unbeknownst to me, I was still in the red zone, where the riptide was. He said, "You'll have to swim to me here. This is as far as I can come." So I kept swimming and kept swimming until I was able to reach his outstretched hand, which he never pulled back until our hands met and his hand closed on mine. He then pulled me into the green zone, lifted me up and out of the water and carried me to the shore. He had to lift me because I could not walk, my leg almost immobilized and swollen and exceedingly painful, but thankfully still there. He took me back past where the water had initially grabbed me and set me down.

It was at that point I remembered Betty. I looked toward the ocean, and they were just helping her out of the water. Apparently she had followed me when I decided to go on without her. Praise God for His wisdom! When she got out, she stood up, came running back to where I was and just collapsed with exhaustion. But she was alive, and she was not even hurt. Praise God for that!

The story might end just there, with both of us making it safely to shore and people helping us, but really the story had just started.

The hospital was closed on Sundays, one of the workers told me. He brought me a golf cart, and we went to the room and put ice on my leg. We had met some people earlier that day and were going to meet them for dinner. Betty said she would stay with me, but I felt this strong desire to be by myself. I knew I wanted to pray out loud and since Betty was not a Christian, I told her to go on. So she helped get me situated and comfortable on the couch, promising to bring me back some food, and then left.

I lay on the couch with my knee swollen and so painful I could hardly touch it. I was afraid it was broken. I had to pack because we were leaving the next morning, and I couldn't even stand. The resort had brought me some crutches, and there I was—tired, weak from the fight and still in shock. I had been attending church for about six months and had been born again. I wanted to sing a song we sang, "I Am a Friend of God," but as I started to hum it, I realized that I couldn't remember the words, the tune or anything. But around me there was music. It was music my pastor's son, Aaron Bagwell, wrote called "Healing in This Place." It says, "There is healing in this place; restoration in this place...." I could hear it as if it were being sung to me. I had my own individual thoughts, such as being unable to remember the words to "I Am a Friend of God", but all the while this music played like a stereo in the room. Then I could see angels lining the room, all around my couch, flying up near the top of the ceiling. They were the ones doing the singing. I don't know how many there were, just that they were in single file lining the perimeter of my room. Well now I know they were standing, but being just new to the way of the Lord, I thought they were flying. They were all wearing white and gold. I don't remember wings or gender, just the most beautiful music I had ever heard. Then I heard a voice—the same voice that began in my stomach, only this time it was behind me and over my right shoulder. The voice told me to put my hands on my knee and confess healing. I just couldn't seem to do it, still searching for the words to "I Am a Friend of God"...so I was struggling with that directive, but I did it anyhow. Then the voice told me He was going to fix it better than it was before.

Well now, I was tired, struggling, watching angels sing, had my hands on my knee and this voice tells me He is going to fix it better than it was before, and it was never broken! How could He possibly fix it better than it was before? Oh, I was angry! I asked Him (not knowing it was the Holy Spirit) how could He fix something that was never broken? "There was nothing wrong with it!" I said aloud to Him. The angels kept singing. I looked at them exasperated. There was silence from Him, and I had never felt silence as loud as I did just at that moment.

Soon the presence of the Lord filled the room. This was shocking to me because I didn't know God could come and fill the room like that. I thought that only happened in church. But no, His presence was so strong, and I felt so good. Everything started to fade and come back to normal just as Betty returned from dinner. So we each had our healing moments.

Three weeks later I was back home and on crutches. My knee had a bad sprain but was not broken. I would leave church early to avoid the crowds because I was in pain. This particular day, I left the church and there was a truck parked right in front of me. The license plate was up high because it was a truck and I was down low because of my crutches. The personalized plate just seemed to jump out at me: "JACOB"; I started crying. I was crying because I knew enough to know that Jacob walked with a limp because he fought with God. I thought I was going to limp because I had fought with God the night of the riptide. I cried and cried and cried. I didn't know how blessed Jacob was at that point or that it was God's way of telling me He was changing my life forever.

Shortly after that, a class was offered for people who had been abused. I took it. What I learned in that class was the Lord's healing ways. I had been laid off, and I couldn't walk but had income from the layoff. Being new in the Lord and hungry to learn more about Him, I used this time to read the Bible, watch Daystar, listen to sermons and attend classes on healing. It was ten solid months of total immersion in the Lord, His Word and His Spirit. What a great time that was for me, in spite of the problems I was going through. I learned about God's healing; how the emotional abuse I encountered had changed me; and how God loved me and chose me, reached down through the waters and put my feet on solid ground and carried me when I could not walk. When I reached out for Him, He took my hand. He not only healed my leg, but my emotions, my scars, my heart and my spirit. He gave me a new job. I never suffered during the whole time I was unemployed. He turned my life around and adopted me into His family.

About a year after the riptide accident, I was quite innocently thanking God for all that He had done my life. He responded in a very soft voice, "That's how I fix things that were never broken." With that one sentence, chills ran through my body. I remembered my attitude toward Him. How I questioned Him. It all came back. I had forgotten, but He hadn't. With that one sentence, I learned to never, never question Him. If He says He's going to fix something that was never broken, then He's going to fix it in dimensions other than the ones you and I know about. He will not only fix things that we know about, He'll fix things we don't know about! His ways are higher than our ways!

—Lind Work

Hope for Freedom

"The Spirit of God, the Master, is on me because God anointed me. He sent me to preach good news to the poor, heal the heartbroken, announce freedom to all captives, pardon all prisoners. God sent me to announce the year of His grace—a celebration of God's destruction of our enemies—and to comfort all who mourn, to care for the needs of all who mourn in Zion, give them bouquets of roses instead of ashes, messages of joy instead of news of doom, a praising heart instead of a languid spirit...." —Isaiah 61:1-3 (The Message)

I AM FIFTY-SIX YEARS OF AGE AND HAVE BEEN MARRIED for thirty-two years. I can say today that I am happy and free, but that has not always been the case.

When I grew up, I suffered much abuse at the hands of my father. I did not understand it at the time, but my relationship with my father was twisted. I saw him more as a "husband" and my role as a "wife," instead of seeing us as father and daughter. My father began abusing me from the time I was a little girl and used me to meet his sexual needs. When my mom and dad divorced, the relationship only intensified. I was expected to play the role of a wife; therefore, I believed that I loved him as a wife would love a husband. It was not until I was fifty years old that I came to understand that my feelings of love for my dad were not healthy, but distorted because of the abuse.

My father used to wake me up at 4:30 A.M. to play tennis before school with him, but I do not remember playing tennis at all. I do remember being very tired and depressed the rest of the day at school. I remember one time my dad stripping me naked in front of servicemen at his tenth-story apartment and my being abused by them. This was during the racial riots in the 1960s in Newark, New Jersey.

Because of the constant abuse, I developed low self-esteem and ran from any challenge that life threw at me. My whole identity was based in shame. I started driving on the highways when I was only eight years old with my dad in the car. At ten years old, I was already six feet tall and very mature looking. I would pick up men while deep inside I did not understand why I was behaving the way I was. I recall one time going with Dad fishing in Lake Hopatcong. I left my dad in the boat and told him I was going to run into town to buy some snacks. I took the car, even though I was not legally allowed to drive because I was underaged. Instead of getting the snacks, I picked up a strange man. We went back to his apartment, but thank God, he found out how old I was and drove me back to where I had left the car. I then went back to where my Dad was fishing and waited until he was done.

As I grew, darkness enveloped me. I came to know Christ and was committed to a great church in Daytona City, Florida, but had yet to find healing and release from my past. I began counseling at my church and came to understand I had dissociative identity disorder. I had learned to deal with the pain and horrific memories of my past by dissociating from them. Over a course of five years of pressing into my Lord Jesus and a lot of counseling, I can say that the darkness is gone and I can experience the goodness and mercy of the Lord which has been following me all the days of my life! Indeed, Jesus is my healer and He has set the captive free!

—Laura Preacher

Hope for the Faithful Giver

"'Bring the whole tithe into the storehouse, so that there may be food in My house, and test Me now in this,' says the Lord of hosts, 'if I will not open for you the windows of heaven and pour out for you a blessing until it overflows.'"

—Malachi 3:10

OUR GIVING JOURNEY STARTED IN 1998, IN A SMALL SPANISH church in Elizabeth, New Jersey. My husband and I were new to the kingdom of God. We remember seeing the great joy on the faces of those who would make their way down the center aisle of the church when they were bringing their gifts to the altar. The worship team played a praise selection that would cause you to jump to your feet! As we observed the joy of the people, we felt compelled to give. We decided that $20 would be an appropriate contribution. We then made our way down and joined the party of givers and made our $20 contribution. This became the offering we gave for a time.

The church we were attending held evening Sunday school classes. My husband and I joined a class regarding finances. It was in the finance class that we learned about tithes and offerings and that 10 percent of our annual gross salary was considered the tithe. We also learned that the offering was anything above the tithe amount. Joy quickly turned into mourning! We were mortified! We were making close to six figures and that would mean our monthly tithes would be a huge chunk of change! We'd never given away that much money before, but we were thankful to God that we went ahead and gave it anyway. We then began our journey to becoming faithful givers.

Every Sunday, we would make our way to church and Pastor would always share the Scriptures with us in Malachi 3, Luke 6:38, and Matthew 6:33. We were always told that blessings would come our way because we became givers and doers of the Word. Yet we were experiencing the very opposite of what we were expecting. The following year, my husband lost his job. Due to disability, I then had to retire from my employment, which I held for twelve years with the company I helped to build. All of a sudden our stable world started to take drastic turns. We were now struggling financially! Even so, we did not quit giving.

It was now close to Christmas and one Sunday, we decided to visit one of our church's sister ministries in downtown Elizabeth that specialized in helping those who were addicted to drugs and alcohol. They were having a special service and asked some of the members of the parent church to attend. We did, and while there, the ministry was requesting an offering. We wrote a check for $50. We were balancing our checkbook the following Monday and realized that we had given the church our last $50! What were we to do? We thought of canceling the check, but the Holy Spirit told us not to. We had to resort to "Plan B"—the change jar. We ran upstairs to get the change jar and made our way to the supermarket and dumped our change into the change machine. By the grace of God, we had $300 in change! That gave us enough money to buy groceries and to put gas in the car. But there was still the matter of Christmas. It was two weeks away, and we had no money. We cried out to God because there was never a Christmas that went by that we could not provide gifts for our children or for each other.

We went to church that following Sunday and got home sometime in the afternoon. In our New Jersey home, we had an enclosed porch. When we arrived home, we found the unexpected. On our porch were two large plastic bags, the kind used up north to collect the dry autumn leaves. They filled to the rim with presents, food and money! The gifts were left to us by perfect strangers! We stood in awe as we went through the bags and found gifts for a boy and a girl (I have one son and one daughter), a turkey with all the boxed sides to complete the Christmas meal, and gift cards so we could buy each other gifts for the holidays. God gave us a spectacular Christmas that year! We understood in a new way that God takes care of His children. He supplies every need!

Since that day, we have been sold out to radically giving into the kingdom of God. We have surpassed the odds in court cases and have won the top awards in every auto case we've had to give to an attorney to handle! We have won against impossible odds with my husband's Social Security case. The attorneys said he was too young to be awarded, yet the favor of God allowed us to win with back pay up to three years and salary payments for life through auto insurance! At the departure of my employment, I was awarded my corporate salary until age sixty-five, along with an approved Social Security case in a record five months! Our most recent victory has been the forgiveness of our home equity line of credit in the amount of $49,927! You cannot out-give God! He does what He says He is going to do! He is true to His Word!

—*Nancy B. Merced*

Hope for the Infirmed

"Let them give thanks to the Lord for His lovingkindness, and for His wonders to the sons of men!" —Psalms 107:21

MY GREAT NEPHEW, MASON, WAS DIAGNOSED WITH neuroblastoma cancer right before his second birthday. He was admitted to Shands Hospital for all the tests and surgery. He then began chemotherapy treatments as his cancer was considered Stage 4. Even though his prognosis was grim, I brought a picture of him to one of our prayer groups and asked that they agree with me that God would move in his situation and healing would come to his body. Our group leader took the picture home with her and committed to pray continually over it.

I am so happy to say Mason just had a complete physical and is cancer-free! He turned five in April and is now starting kindergarten! Prayer really works! I hope this brings encouragement to someone else going through cancer. God is still in the healing business!

—Kathy C.

Hope for a Fresh Start

"Behold, the former things have come to pass, now I declare new things; before they spring forth I proclaim them to you."

—Isaiah 42:9

MY NAME IS DENISE. I'M FORTY-TWO YEARS OLD AND currently reside in Orlando, Florida. Back in 1997, I went through a horrible divorce with an abusive husband. I was living in Killeén, Texas at the time, with two children. My daughter was seven and my son was fifteen months. Since I had family in Clearwater, Florida, I decided to move back home to be closer to them.

At that time, I had only a high school education. I had always dreamed of becoming a nurse, but I never had the money to go back to school or the backing of my ex-husband. I ended up moving into public housing in Clearwater. I went to St. Petersburg Junior College full time and worked part time as a Certified Nursing Assistant, all the while raising my two children alone.

I graduated from St. Petersburg Junior College in May 2000 with my associate's degree in nursing, and passed my RN boards. I was able to move out of public housing that year into my own apartment. I then enrolled at the University of South Florida and graduated in May 2002 with my BSN. I continued my education and ultimately graduated from The University of Tampa with a master's degree in nursing in August 2006.

I am currently a nurse practitioner with a neurosurgery group in Orlando, at Florida Hospital. My daughter is now twenty-three and my son will be seventeen in November. I was able to accomplish all of this as a single mom with hard work and, of course, through the grace of God. I love to help other women who find themselves in the same situation that I have been in. God is able to make all things new, and give a fresh start!

—Denise Holloway

Hope for Wholeness

"Though the cherry trees don't blossom and the strawberries don't ripen, though the apples are worm-eaten and the wheat fields stunted, though the sheep pens are sheepless and the cattle barns empty, I'm singing joyful praise to God. I'm turning cartwheels of joy to my Savior God. Counting on God's Rule to prevail, I take heart and gain strength. I run like a deer. I feel like I'm king of the mountain!..." —Habakkuk 3:17-19 (The Message)

AT THE AGE OF FIVE YEARS OLD, I WAS MOLESTED BY MY babysitter and her son. You may ask how that could have happened. My babysitter would take me into her teenage son's room and allow him to sexually abuse me.

I do not remember how long the abuse lasted, but it went on for a long time. When they were finished, she would give me a bath and prepare my siblings and me to be picked up by my parents.

Growing up, I suppressed the memories as much as I could. I had not told anyone about the abuse until a couple of years ago. Even then, I still tried to suppress it even more.

Although I was molested, my childhood overall wasn't horrible. I found it difficult to enjoy it and it was hard growing up. I grew up quickly and felt as if it was my duty to protect my siblings and other children from harm. I was afraid to be around men alone and was afraid for any child to be around a man alone. I did not hang out with children my age for the most part. I grew up hanging around adults.

It wasn't until I left for college that the memory of the abuse started to unveil itself in full force. I had become even more horrified being in places alone and also around other men alone. At one time during that period, I almost gave up on the gift inside of me that God had given. I started having nightmares on a regular basis. I had gotten to the point where I felt like I could no longer cope, and left school. When I left school, I gave the excuse that finances determined my decision for leaving. In actual fact, it was fear. Finances were not the issue, as I knew God would have taken care of my finances.

After leaving college, I went through a lot of struggles. I even contemplated suicide. The thing is, through the midst of all of this, God still kept me. What is even more amazing is that He kept me even when I did not want to be kept. He shielded me and covered me throughout my life. My life could have gone downhill after I was molested, and it could have especially gone downhill after I left college. I was and I still am covered by His love.

I am almost in my mid-twenties, and I can say that God has allowed me to walk a life of purity and abstinence. I am saving myself for marriage.

Though I have come a long way from that frightened little girl, I know that I still have a long way to go. The fantastic thing is, God has taught me and is still teaching me how to worship Him in spirit and truth—not just with my words, but with my life. He has taught me and is continuing to teach me how to walk a pure life before Him, even in the midst of life's storms that come my way.

With all of that being said, God has surrounded me with wonderful people who teach sound biblical doctrine, who walk in excellence, who truly love God and desire to do what is right and who truly love me for who I am! No matter what our struggles are in life, we no longer have to ask God, "Why me?"—although sometimes we still do. I am working on asking God, "Why *not* me?" I am thankful that I am coming to a place of true wholeness!

—Camia Berry

Hope for His Provision

"Now to Him who is able to do far more abundantly beyond all that we ask or think, according to the power that works within us, to Him be the glory..." —Ephesians 3:20-21

IN 2011 WE BEGAN TO LOSE CLIENTS IN OUR BUSINESS, AND were not as busy as we used to be. Our auto detailing business was our main source of income, and not getting enough business was troubling to us. This caused us to default on our financial obligations, especially our mortgage payments. We began to have months of late payments and then no payments at all; at which point we received a letter from our current mortgage company that our home was going to be foreclosed on.

My wife and I were overwhelmed with fear and did not know what to do. There was no way out, and the situation seemed impossible. When we received a letter stating that the house was indeed in foreclosure, it sent us into a panic mode. Questions arose in our hearts such as where were we going to go with our children? We were desperate for answers and solutions. We immediately started praying and asking God what to do. The Lord guided us to call one of our clients who happened to be an attorney. We were going to him for advice on what to do. This attorney client of ours referred us to another attorney for legal advice. We were hoping that he could assist us to postpone the foreclosure proceedings. However, the attorney charged us $2,500 to take care of filing papers to stall the foreclosure. We did not have the money and even with a payment plan, we still did not know where we would get it. The attorney was going to attempt to delay the process for about ten to twelve months without us needing to make a payment. We had to trust God. By His grace, God provided the payments for the attorney to file the necessary papers.

Meanwhile, our business remained the same, with little or no resources. With all that we faced, we remained committed to sowing and paying our tithes. We even raised our tithe from 10 percent to 11 percent.

We had to believe God with everything in us, knowing that the only way out was through faith. We had to trust God to deliver us. Before we knew it, the twelve-month extension had gone by. We received a phone call from our attorney stating that another mortgage company had picked up our mortgage and was now making an offer to us.

We never applied for a loan modification, and we were wondering what this really meant. We had missed the call from the attorney, and we became overwhelmed with fear and anxiety. Confused about what to do, we felt at a loss for words. We were not sure what to expect when we returned the attorney's phone call. We had no money, no family members who could help us, and no place to go. Our only option was to cry out to God for help. When we finally summoned the courage to respond to the attorney, little did we know that there was about to be a shift.

As we held our breath, the attorney proceeded to advise us that he wished what had just taken place had happened to him personally. He then advised us that a new mortgage company had picked up our mortgage loan. They were making an offer to us, and even though currently our interest rate was 8.9 percent, the new mortgage company was willing to bring it down to 3.9 percent. Also, our mortgage payment was $1,700, and they were willing to bring it down to $1,100. Not only that, but the current principle was $239,000, but the mortgage company reduced it to $135,000 with a huge difference of $104,000! The late fees, which included taxes and penalties, were about $27,000. The mortgage company offered us a loan modification, which we never asked for nor applied for!

The reason we did not even think to go this route was because there was no way we could ever qualify for this type of loan due to the fact that our credit was messed up. This most definitely was a miracle of God which neither we, nor the attorney had ever seen before. The difference of $104,000 plus the $27,000 were totally wiped off. As if this was not enough, we were also advised that we were in good standing and there was no outstanding debt! We were miraculously caught up with everything—taxes, payments and all. This, of course, is the incredible work of God, and we were just in awe of His goodness.

We were completely astonished and very grateful that He had saved our home, which He had blessed us with. However, shortly after this incredible testimony of God's hand moving miraculously in our situation, God moved again.

Now that we were back on track with our payments, we, by His grace, had successfully made two payments. It was a bit of a challenge to do so, however, God provided yet again. We were still trusting God all the way and believing Him to take care of us on a month-to-month basis because our business was still a bit unstable.

Unknown to us, God was still working behind the scenes to assist us and to do that which only He could do. My wife was calling the automated payment system for our mortgage to make the next payment when something unusual occurred. She discovered that even though our monthly mortgage payment was $1,121, there was already a payment made in the amount of $1,435. Obviously, it showed an additional $314 which was a separate payment made to the principal. Let me state that this payment was definitely not made by me, nor by my wife. How this payment was made and who made it remains a big mystery. Even with my wife calling the automated system three times, the operator two times and going on the account history online, she still could not figure out how this payment could have been made. We were left with the conclusion that this was the hand of God supernaturally moving on our behalf.

This experience and powerful outcome have taught us to trust God because He is always faithful and His goodness and mercy follow us all the days of our lives. When He promises to supply all our needs according to His riches in glory through Christ Jesus, it is absolutely true in more ways than we can ever imagine. Our God is good and we are confident that there is more to come!

—Teva Batani

Hope for a Blessing

"Then Jacob was left alone, and a man wrestled with him until daybreak. When he saw that he had not prevailed against him, he touched the socket of his thigh; so the socket of Jacob's thigh was dislocated while he wrestled with him. Then he said, 'Let me go, for the dawn is breaking.' But he said, 'I will not let you go unless you bless me.' So he said to him, 'What is your name?' And he said, 'Jacob.' He said, 'Your name shall no longer be Jacob, but Israel; for you have striven with God and with men and have prevailed.'" —Genesis 32:24-28

MY BISHOP OFTEN SAYS THAT NO ONE ESCAPES THIS LIFE without experiencing some sort of emotional or psychological wound. The most painful of these wounds, the father wound, can be especially impactful because of the affirming role that fathers play in our life development. In my story, I can trace one of my greatest victories of spiritual growth to a moment when God awakened me to see a wound as a blessing, a fall as a chance to restart, and a failure as an opportunity for intimacy with Him.

In 1994, I had moved out of my childhood home in Orlando, Florida and moved to Chicago for five years. Although I had grown up in a typical "PK" (preacher's kid) home, I was making some important life decisions and not always using the sound judgment that my father had exemplified in our home. One of these decisions resulted in me having to make the most difficult phone call of my life as I had to explain that I would soon be a single parent. This was obviously not in my life script, and the horror of coming clean with this truth was more than I could bear. As I wept bitter tears over the phone, I could almost see a scowl of disappointment come across the face of my father.

Being a strict disciplinarian, this was a look I was all too familiar with, as I had often seen it after a not-so-stellar report card or during a yelling session following many fights my brother and I would engage in as boys struggling for the place of favorite son. But this time, I felt that there was nothing I could say or do that would make this right. The only thing more painful than having to explain my current predicament was the next thing I would hear him say. After a long pause and a couple of deep breaths, my father said, "Well...God will forgive you, but your ministry will always have a limp to it, and you'll have to deal with this for the rest of your life."

Those words felt like a punch to my gut, and their echo would affect how I would receive the grace of God in the midst of my grief. After this conversation, I would project my feelings of "father disappointment" to my heavenly Father and would make it harder for Him to fully restore me to my full potential for many years to come.

With this damaged mindset, I limped through the next ten years encountering only glimpses of greatness while I served from the bottom up in every role of church ministry in search of my place in the family of God once again. Then one day during one of the darkest seasons of my entire life, an old Bible story came alive with new meaning in a way that only God could speak. Freedom and confidence are dream-feeders, and these would be the key ingredients I would need to gain a new perspective of my purpose in the kingdom.

The story was the well-known account of Jacob's blessing and the wrestling match with the angel that would forever change his identity and destiny. As I read the account of Genesis 32:24-31, I noticed right away that Jacob had gotten himself to a place of solitude and surrender. Although I had been exposed to solid preaching, amazing worship and anointed ministry experiences, I too found myself ready to give it all up for something more authentic and a more genuine relationship with God not based on works, but truth. The Bible doesn't explain what started the wrestling match, but Jacob's goal was clear in verse 26: "*I will not let you go unless you bless me.*" I came to understand that the blessing I had wrestled for all these years was approval and validation. I wanted this from my dad, but at the most painful moment of my life, all I seemed to receive was disappointment and disillusionment.

In the story, Jacob's struggle can only end when he accepts the fact that he can't turn the corner of this season in his life until he surrenders the very thing he thinks he's fighting for—his identity. Jacob has to die in order for Israel to be born. Since the struggle wouldn't end on its own, the angel had to give him a limp that would then engage him in a new conversation not based on what Jacob wanted, but on what he needed. What I came to understand was that my limp was not the stigma of single parenthood that would disqualify me from my call, but rather, it was proof that I had been in a real struggle and God's touch was going to be forever evident in the very thing that had once hurt me. God's dream for my life and my identity could only be found in who I was in *His* eyes, not in what others said or dreamt for me.

In fact, for better or worse, my identity wasn't even based on the persona that I had grown up to be. This crisis had not come to destroy me, but to reveal who I really was and to create a unique invitation to become the person God meant for me to be all along. It wasn't until I was ready to trade my sorrows and pain that I could take on the joy of the Lord.

My story is one of rebirth and true approval and validation from the One who knew me before I even knew myself. What my earthly father said may have appeared to be a physical assessment of my moral failure, but in actuality, it was a declaration that I would one day wrestle until I could wrestle no more, and my "injury" would become a catalyst for a new dance I would have with the Angel who held my new name and destiny on His lips. Once He declared who I really was, and once I embraced that new name, I was free to be fully intimate with Him at a level I had never known before.

Today, even though I felt as though I had to reset my destiny clock, I no longer struggle with approval and validation, as those are blessings that the Lord granted me quite some time ago. I'm doing the things that I thought I would never do and God has more than replaced my identity—He's given me a great story...His story that continues to unfold in my walk with the Lord.

By the way, my dad and I have a much better relationship, and we celebrate approval and validation in who we are in Christ every day.

—Juan Aviles

Hope Fulfilled

"Then you would trust, because there is hope; and you would look around and rest securely." —Job 11:18

MY HUSBAND AND I HAD BEEN MARRIED APPROXIMATELY twenty years when we built our dream home. I was so excited and we were blessed to be able to decorate the inside of our home just the way we wanted to. It was absolutely beautiful! As a woman, I love my home and feel as though it is a reflection of who I am on the inside. I desire everyone who enters our home to feel welcome and at peace.

We have a beautiful swimming pool outside on a covered porch area. The space was larger than the home we moved from and it was the one area that I didn't have the proper furniture for to complete the desired look. Because of the great expense of building and furnishing our home, my husband told me to wait for the outdoor furniture. I tried my best to be patient, but every few months I would ask him if we could afford to purchase the furniture for the pool area yet. He always said not quite yet. This went on for about five years.

One day when I asked if it was time yet, he surprised me by answering that he thought we could afford to purchase the outdoor furniture. I was so excited! We set aside a Saturday afternoon and went to our favorite furniture/patio store. I knew exactly what I wanted; it took no time to work with a sales lady to put together the set that I felt would finish off my home perfectly. I picked out an outdoor couch, two lounge chairs, two end tables and a coffee table. I even found an outdoor rug to finish the look off! I felt like all my dreams were falling right into place! That is until she rang up the total for what I had picked. She came back with her calculator and had a smile on her face as she internally calculated her commission. She then told us that our total would be $20,000. I thought I was going to die and instantly saw my dream evaporate into thin air!

We left the store without the furniture and I felt as though I would never have what was in my heart. My husband then informed me that I was to leave it alone and not ask him about patio furniture anymore. I understood, but felt defeated. While I was praying one day, I felt the Lord challenge me to ask Him for the desire of my heart. I had never stretched my faith before to believe Him for something that expensive when I knew it was a luxury and not a necessity. I was also challenged because I knew I could not ask my husband to provide the furniture for me, so I had to completely rely on God to work a miracle for me. So I boldly told the Lord, "OK. I can't ask my husband for the patio furniture, so I am going to ask You for it." I then would remind the Lord every few days that I was believing Him to provide me with patio furniture; but I said nothing to my husband about it—which any woman can attest to is not an easy thing to do!

After a few months of asking the Lord for my furniture, my husband came to me one day and said he was on the phone with a friend who had been helping someone decorate their new home. His client had ordered patio furniture but did not like it when it arrived. It was a custom order, but she did not like the color. Instead of returning the furniture and having the upholstery changed, she decided to put it into storage and buy something completely different. He told my husband that the set was sitting in a storage bin not ever having been used. My husband told him that I had been looking for a set of patio furniture and to inquire of his client if she was willing to sell it to us. Our friend did just that but came back to us a few days later and told us that his client said we could have the furniture and it would not cost us a dime! My husband came back to me and asked me if I wanted it. Sight unseen, I knew God was answering my prayers and told him to have it delivered to our home.

Within the week, a van pulled into our driveway and patio furniture was being unloaded. I could not believe the goodness of God! The furniture matched our décor perfectly! Not only that, but there was enough furniture to beautifully decorate the entire space including two outdoor areas that were not under the covered patio! God had answered my prayers above and beyond even what I had been asking Him for! I can only imagine how much all the furniture cost because I knew how out of reach just the fraction of what was given to us was worth!

God taught me a valuable lesson through all of this. Not only did He teach me to trust Him to provide for even my most intimate desires and not think that I had to receive that provision only through my husband, but that when He answers, He goes beyond what I could have ever imagined because He loves me that much!

—R. E. C.

Hope for the Empty-Nester

"Train up a child in the way he should go, even when he is old, he will not depart from it." —Proverbs 22:6

IT'S SOMETHING TO SEE A GROWN MAN FIGHTING BACK TEARS. My son's father struggled mightily to contain his emotions as the three of us rode down the elevator together, in silence before we said good-bye.

"I've been dreading this day," he had told me. And now it was here.

There had been a steady stream of parents and students in and out of the dorm building all day long, pushing pull-cars loaded with rubber cartons and cardboard boxes filled with what would make their dorm rooms feel like home. They, like me, had prepared, by making multiple trips to Target and Wal-Mart for toiletries, laundry baskets and pop tarts.

But I wondered how many of them would be going from a broken home to an empty nest.

You see, my son's father and I divorced when our son was eleven months old. I had raised my son alone, fully aware of what the statistics say about African-American males raised in single-parent households: that they have a better chance of being high school dropouts or prison inmates than college freshmen.

As a former news anchor, I would often report on these "facts," then go home to a curly-haired, brown-eyed little boy who needed his mommy. What the media would say about a child like mine would break my heart. I prayed that drugs, babies' mommas, prison or premature death would not become my son's reality.

I made some hard decisions over the years, choosing to leave a prestigious job in television news, to work for less money and little status, so I could spend more time with my son. And even though I remarried when my son started high school, I maintained communication with my ex-husband, allowing him to see his son whenever he wanted. And to this day I am beyond grateful that my son's father stepped up with child support payments that always arrived on time, not to mention Saturday morning trips to the zoo, sleepovers and afternoons at the park with his boy. He coached our son's football and basketball teams, and sat for hours on hard metal bleachers watching countless high school track meets. He was there the day our son became a state champion, and he showed up an hour early for his high school graduation ceremony.

And here he was again on college move-in day.

Though divorced and living separately, we had managed to put our adult differences aside for the sake of our son. And that was the difference maker. Though "broken," our family behaved as if we were whole.

And so now, I'm an empty-nester, and I can't cry. Yes, I had a lump in my throat as we said good-bye and I drove off the college campus, headed toward an empty house. A few warm liquid beads formed at the corner of my eyes and spilled with little plops onto my shoulder. But that was it. I couldn't cry. Because this is what we had been working toward all these years. This is what all those parent-teacher conferences and curriculum nights were all about, the cartons of Crayolas and mechanical pencils, book nook, and parent nights, the piles of registration forms and fees, campus tours and college entrance exams, church camp and Sunday school.

This was why.

And today, deep down inside of me, I know we're not alone. Right now there are African-American young men on college campuses all over this country just like my son. Whether the leader of the free world and an Ivy League graduate living at the most prestigious address in the northern hemisphere, or a gangly 19-year-old calling a state university dorm room the size of a storage locker *home,* the "statistics" lie.

I chose not to focus on statistics, but to stand on the Word. Somewhere a long time ago, I read what the Scriptures said: *"Train up a child in the way that they should go and in the end they will not depart from it"* (see Proverbs 22:6). While that's not a guarantee that everything will work out in the end, it was enough for me to build my hope upon.

Just weeks after my son left home he called me on a Sunday night and we started chatting about how his classes were going and how he was adjusting to college life. He told me about his professors and his track coaches, and talked about his favorite places on campus to eat. He also told me how he was having trouble sleeping because of the college kids roaming the dorm room halls at two and three o'clock in the morning. He talked about how annoyed he was with the drinking and loud partying; and then he said this: "Thank you. Thank you, Mom. Now I understand why you raised me the way you did."

Yes, I'm an empty-nester, but I can't cry. Because after years of feathering my nest with the Word of God, I find solace and great joy in knowing that despite the "statistics," the life of my young black male child has just started to hatch.

—*Roxane Battle Morrison*

Hope for Our Safety

"You will not be afraid of the terror by night, or of the arrow that flies by day; of the pestilence that stalks in darkness, or of the destruction that lays waste at noon. A thousand may fall at your side and ten thousand at your right hand; but it shall not approach you." —Psalms 91:5-7

MY STORY COMES FROM THE ARCHIVES OF MY YOUNGER DAYS. I am a visually-limited person and found myself flying from Alberta, Canada to Munich, Germany unaccompanied. Navigating the Munich train station was a strong incentive for continuous prayer. As I tried to figure out where I should go, I met a man who was very helpful and got me to the right platform to catch the train to the little town of Hurlach, where the YWAM castle was located.

This was the location for teams helping to prepare for the Munich Olympic Games' outreach.

I expected my "friend" to say, "Good-bye," and leave, but he stayed sitting beside me on the platform and, moving closer, asked me in broken German for a kiss. I began praying urgently inside and moved the other way. At this point, a young man with long hair and a guitar appeared on the otherwise deserted platform. He asked if I spoke English and to my "Yes," he exclaimed, "Praise the Lord!" To which I replied the same thing with great joy! He sat down on my other side, and we began chatting like long lost friends. He was also headed to the castle. The unwanted "friend" lost interest in me and left. I am not sure how I would have arrived safely to the castle without this strange answer to my urgent prayer. God is indeed our shield and our protector!

—Alma Siemens

Hope in the One Who Will Help in the Time of Need

"Why are you in despair, O my soul? And why are you disturbed within me? Hope in God, for I shall again praise Him, the help of my countenance, and my God."

—Psalms 43:5

I HAVE BEEN DIAGNOSED WITH CANCER FIVE TIMES OVER THE last thirty-six months. My desire is to tell people never to give up!

I have had six surgeries in thirty-six months. My left kidney was removed because it was full of cancer. I have had cancer three times in the bladder with surgery and chemotherapy each time. Cancer was also found in the tubes running from my right kidney to my bladder. Along with all of this, I had to undergo surgery for a hernia.

Through all of these trials, I never gave up, and as of February 4, 2013, all of my tests show that I am cancer-free!

On top of all that, during this process, I did not have any insurance, money or a job; but God provided and met all my needs! He indeed is good!

—Roberto Bolanos

Hope for a New Beginning

"Therefore if anyone is in Christ, he is a new creature; the old things passed away; behold, new things have come."
—II Corinthians 5:17

I HAD COME TO A PLACE OF HOPELESSNESS ABOUT TWENTY years ago and was going to commit suicide. I had tried everything to make myself feel better, from making money, to different relationships and even being bulimic for fourteen years. But nothing helped. I was married to my second husband thinking that love was the missing piece in my life, only to end up fighting constantly. I thought that marriage would change all of that, but it didn't.

I had four children going into my second marriage and my husband had four children of his own. We would have five of our children every other weekend because they were very young at the time, and they were in the midst of all of this constant strife. It was just awful. My husband and I had gone to marriage counselors and psychiatrists to try and fix our relationship, but nothing helped. The psychiatrists told my husband that he should just leave me because he would never be able to have a life with me. They said I was schizophrenic, and they wanted to put me on medication and in an institution.

I had suffered depression, was filled with anxiety and fear and could not hold down a job. I didn't want to go on any medication, and I certainly didn't want to go into an institution. When I divorced my first husband, I felt like my children were better off living with their dad because I could barely take care of myself.

After my second husband, Frank, and I separated, he would call me every once in a while, and I would just hang up on him because I was so angry. Frank was a Vietnam veteran and had a lot of anger, which he expressed outwardly. I, on the other hand, kept everything inside, which ultimately led to my depression.

One Saturday after a month of being separated, a very depressed Frank called me. I had never heard him sound so desperate, and he said he wanted to come home. I felt really badly for him. So, I told him to come back home because I thought that he would be different. I was wrong. Nothing changed between us and the fighting continued. All I wanted was to be loved. One night I was so frustrated and upset that I took a cross with Jesus on it that was hanging over our bed (I was raised Catholic) and brought it with me to a lake in Bolton, Connecticut. I was crying, and I asked Jesus to help me because I didn't know what else to do. Money didn't make me happy, men didn't make me happy, having children didn't help me—nothing helped!

Little did I realize that Jesus was listening. A few nights after that, Frank and I had a huge fight. He stormed out of the house and drove away, and I was just crying. I told myself, "That is it. I can't take it anymore. I'm just going to kill myself." In my heart I didn't want to end it all, but I didn't know what else to do. I looked over at our phone, and I saw a business card from the Christian Fellowship Center located in Bristol, Connecticut. Frank's friend had given the card to him because he and his wife had counseled with Pastor Herb Desjardins from that church for their own marriage, but Frank never paid attention to it. Somehow the card ended up by our phone, so I picked up the phone and called the number. Pastor Herb answered the phone, and I was still crying. I told him that I didn't want to live anymore and had tried everything to make me happy, but nothing worked. He invited me to come to one of their healing services.

So, when my husband came home that night, I told him that I had called the number on the business card and that the pastor had invited me to a healing service. I asked Frank if he would like to go with me, and he said he would.

In 1993, we went to the healing service and gave our lives to Jesus. That is when the healing began. I began volunteering at the church, helping them wherever they needed help. It was great because it got the focus off of my hurt and my pain, and I saw how many lives were being helped through the services the church had to offer.

Man couldn't put me or my marriage back together, but God did. Little by little, as I applied myself to counseling, took part in the support groups, and volunteered, the Lord began healing me and restoring our marriage. I even ran the soup kitchen and food pantry for seven years, when they said I would never be able to hold down a job!

Now I am the Promotional Director of the Christian Fellowship Center. Not only that, but my husband and I celebrated our twentieth anniversary last October, and lead marriage support groups at the church. What a miracle! There is nothing that is impossible for the Lord and nothing that He cannot fix! We have a poster at our church that says, "'Dear Jesus, I have a problem...it's me.' 'Dear Child, I have the answer...it's Me.'"

—Michelle Palmer

Hope for Finances

"Sing praises to the Lord, which dwelleth in Zion: declare among the people his doings....For the needy shall not always be forgotten: the expectation of the poor shall not perish forever."
—Psalms 9:11,18 (KJV)

IN 1995, I BECAME A SINGLE MOM. I HAD BEEN OUT OF the workforce for two years and had two children—a two-year-old, and a three-year-old. It didn't take me long to find a job that paid a little over minimum wage. I was sitting at my desk at work one day and I came across an article that stated that over 80 percent of single parents live under the poverty line.

It wasn't long before I was living that reality. I moved back into my parents' house with two kids in tow, and had $14 left in the bank with two weeks left before payday. I was at a lifetime low. Just when I thought it couldn't get much worse my daughter came home begging me to buy her a new pair of boots, because the kids at school were teasing her about the ones she was wearing. The boots she wanted were $12. At that point I realized there was not much difference between having $14 or $2 and watching her anguish disappear was worth it.

It was that day that I made a determination that I was not going to remain another poverty line statistic. I enrolled in the university and completed a five-year program in four years. Graduating with a double major, I was sure I could take care of my family. Only upon graduation, I couldn't find a job in my field. I was unemployed for one year when I took a job for a nonprofit youth organization that paid less than I was making before I had two degrees.

I lived at my parents' house for one year, and saved up enough money to put a down payment on a small place; but I still didn't feel like I was making enough money to take care of my family. I cried out to God; I was angry, hurt and confused. I thought, "I didn't just spend four years in school to be making less money than I was making before!"

I heard Him speak to my heart, "I am your provider. Do you trust Me?" Oh how I wanted to trust Him; but I didn't.

Remembering the story in Mark 9:24, I cried out again, "Lord, forgive my unbelief!" With that I purchased a four- bedroom townhouse that needed a lot of work. Within six months of the purchase of that condo the housing market jumped and I sold the property for a $50,000 profit. Now it was time to buy another house. However, I ran into an obstacle. I could not buy another house. The bank would not even give me an appointment to see a banker, because they did not think I made enough money to qualify for a mortgage.

That same week a gentleman I had never met before came into our offices at the youth organization to make a donation. Somehow we began talking and I told him the story about the bank not being willing to even give me an appointment. The man handed me his card and told me to come see him. He was a mortgage broker. He sold mortgages for the bank and had a zero percent default reputation. Not one mortgage he had ever sold had defaulted. I went to meet with him and he said, "It appears that the bank is right, you do not qualify for a mortgage. However, I feel like I am supposed to do everything in my power to help you, so I will grant you a mortgage, based on my reputation."

I was ecstatic. That month I had bought my first single-dwelling home. Shortly after that, due to unforeseen circumstances, the nonprofit organization shut down and I was once again unemployed.

We spent a year living off of savings and credit. Again I cried out to God. Again I was angry, hurt, confused, and I felt His gentle strong voice ask me, "Do you trust Me?" Again I begged Him to forgive my unbelief.

That week, a young man at my church who was a customer service manager at the bank, offered me a position as a teller, only because he had compassion on me, and I used to be his youth pastor. Unfortunately, the job only paid $11.25 an hour; once again a job that paid less than I was making before I had two degrees!

I complained to the Lord, "Come on! I have two degrees. Surely You can provide a job that pays more than $11 an hour." Again, even in my rebellious murmurings, He kept speaking to my heart, "I am your provider, and if you are going to complain, at least get it right; it's $11.25 an hour." I laughed and I cried and He spoke to me through First Thessalonians 5:17-18: *"pray continually, give thanks in all circumstances, for this is God's will for you in Christ Jesus"* (NIV).

So I did. I kept my $11.25 an hour job and continually gave thanks for it. After working at the bank for three months, I was promoted to financial advisor. Shortly after my promotion I married my best friend. Less than one year after we married I felt in my heart that we were to purchase a house that was well beyond our budget. However, I had learned something in the past ten years; trust God, pray continually, and give thanks in all circumstances.

My husband's and my income combined could not qualify us for the purchase price of this house. My husband calculated all the numbers and they did not work; we simply could not afford this house. I didn't care, I felt the Lord telling me to try. So we tried. At that time I was still employed at the bank, still making less than I did before I had two degrees; nevertheless, as an employee, the bank waived the income requirements and allowed us to purchase the house. That $11.25 an hour job had finally paid off! Not only that, but the Lord provided a renter for the original house. The rent paid that mortgage as well as a portion of the mortgage of the new house.

Once I put my trust in God, He began to open doors for me to use my education. I began receiving contract work and made more money in two weeks than I made in an entire year. Still, He continues to ask me, "Do you trust Me?"

Today, I am happily married, with not two, but three kids; not one, but two houses; not one, but two cars; and we had a dog, but he had to go! The combined value of the homes is over $1.5 million, and the equity in the homes is over $1 million.

There were many people who were in my same situation ten years ago, and they are still in the same situation today. I had a choice to make: to put my trust in myself and my education, or trust God. It is much more fun to trust God, and it is easier to be a God-made millionaire than a man-made one.

—Nanette Lucas

Hope for the Widowed

"The Lord will destroy the house of the proud: but he will establish the border of the widow." —Proverbs 15:25 (KJV)

MY HUSBAND OF FORTY-SEVEN YEARS DIED OF LUNG CANCER. We lived at our last home for thirty-eight years where we had done many things together. I felt the Lord speak to my heart about nine months after Jim's death that it would be difficult for me to start a new life while living in my husband's shadow. I told the Lord that if He wanted me to move, I would be willing.

I told two people the next day that I would be selling my home, and they both wanted to buy it. I chose my neighbor. I was a little surprised because I thought it would take much longer for my home to sell, but God isn't one to wait around.

Since I felt it was God's idea for me to make this move, I decided to tell Him where I would like to live and what I would like to have in my new home. I told Him the exact location where I wanted to live and that I would like a fenced-in yard for my dog, high ceilings, a fireplace, walk-in closet and one and a half baths. The first house I looked at was exactly where I had asked to be and had everything in it I had asked for— and more! The sellers had just lowered the price to $125,000, which is what I had sold my home for. My niece offered them $117,000, they took it and I could move right in. She also handled all the paperwork so I didn't have to pay a realtor. We closed on both homes an hour apart on the same day; which I hear is very unusual.

I have a small women's Bible study in my home, and I was going to cancel it so I could clean the carpets before I moved in, but I decided to put God first and have the Bible study anyway. Two hours after the Bible study, two other friends came over with their carpet cleaners and cleaned all my carpets for me! Several of my friends gathered together and moved all my belongings for me. All I had to do was tell them where to set my things.

I love my new home and consider it a gift from God. I also have prayed for years for Christian neighbors and I even have those! I thank God constantly for His love and grace which brought me here and how He has blessed me for the past six years. God is no respecter of persons. What He has done for me, He will do for you, if you ask!

—*Claudia Reynolds*

Hope for Help in the Valley of the Shadow of Death

"Yea, though I walk through the valley of the shadow of death, I will fear no evil: for thou art with me...." —Psalms 23:4 (KJV)

SOME YEARS AGO, WHILE DRIVING WITH MY WIFE, I MADE a left turn at an intersection and did not see the oncoming car. We were "T-boned," our car was totaled and knocked into a service station parking area. The impact was shocking as the other car didn't have time to brake before hitting us. Despite the seat belts, we were jostled around the front seat quite a bit.

After gathering ourselves and making sure we were OK, we got out of the car, checked on the other car and waited for law enforcement to arrive. People instantly gathered around and were talking with each other quite a lot. When the police arrived to investigate the accident, the officer asked me if we were the only people in my car. I replied, "Yes, just my wife and me." Instantly the crowd became extremely vocal as they shouted correction to my statement to the officer. "No," they shouted, "There was another man who was driving the car. He got out after the wreck and walked away."

They were so insistent that it was very difficult to prove to the officer that my wife and I were the only passengers in the car. The crowd was never convinced. They insisted they saw a man walk away, but no one could say where he went!

We can only believe it was an Angel of the Lord that protected us from harm, perhaps even death. Most felt that any car hit that hard would have caused serious injuries, but we walked away. We say, "Praise the Lord for His protection."

—Gerald Doggett

Hope for Divine Healing

"[Jesus] called his twelve disciples to him and gave them authority to drive out evil spirits and to heal every disease and sickness." —Matthew 10:1 (NIV)

OVER THE COURSE OF THREE MONTHS, MY SISTER HAS seen God's mighty hand of healing grace. She attended an appointment for an annual mammogram in November 2012 and the test results revealed a mass density that depleted the red blood cells. This resulted in numerous tests to confirm the presence of cancer cells. The doctor indicated that they had to detect the source and prime location of the cancer. He also told her that within the last couple of hours, seven of his patients had test results return positive with breast cancer.

Knowing our mighty God is a healer, we immediately began to pray earnestly while the many tests continued. After the last MRI scan showed two mass areas of concern, the doctor quickly changed the date of surgery from February 4, 2013 to January 29, 2013. She was told that this would be a one-hour outpatient surgery for a mastectomy and would require and an hour for the plastic surgeon.

Again, we saw God's hand at work and continued earnestly praying for a miracle. God indeed showed up and performed a miracle for my sister. The surgeon shared that they removed a portion of the tissue surrounding the mass and were able to leave tissue that was absolutely normal, along with extra skin for the plastic surgeon to enhance the area. There was also removal of lymph nodes for testing, which also appeared to be normal. After surgery, my sister was transferred to Recovery—with pain, but blessed!

The next day, with restrictions, my sister was out of bed and stirring around! On February 4th and 5th, she accomplished follow-up with both doctors and each revealed that the test results from the lab returned normal. We are continuously giving thanks and praying that the doctor's statement, "...unsure if she will need chemotherapy..." turns out to be that she is completely healed and will not require any more treatment. We know our heavenly Father is a healer, and nothing is too hard for Him!

—Rose Mary Banks

Hope in the One Who Meets All Our Needs

"...Fear not: believe only, and she shall be made whole."
—Luke 8:50 (KJV)

I WAS A SINGLE MOTHER RAISING TWO CHILDREN ON A SMALL salary. I did not ever accept any type of assistance from the government. It never really entered my mind to do so. There were times when we struggled, but I always kept my faith in God. I would pray the same prayer every day: "Lord, give me strength to do what I need to do." He gave it abundantly! I would work from 9:00 A.M. to 6:00 P.M. every day. On Fridays, I worked until 6:00 P.M., slept three hours, got ready for my weekend job and went to work from 11:30 P.M. until 11:30 the next morning. My day off was what was left of Sunday. Someone would constantly leave notes on my door about working on Sundays. I ignored those notes and kept doing what I needed to do.

The Lord gave me the strength to do this for ten years, but two years ago I started having extremely heavy monthly cycles. By the time I went to the doctor, it was almost too late. He thought I would need a blood transfusion. I prayed and gave my situation to God. Another doctor told me that I needed a hysterectomy. I was told that I would have to have money up front in order for him to perform the surgery. I did not have the money, so I gave it to God. I prayed and asked the Lord to either provide the money for the surgery or to lessen the bleeding. He answered my prayers and lessened the bleeding! He is faithful to take care of us no matter what we go through! Our God is a healing God and an awesome provider!

—Susie Lloyd

Hope in Times of the Seemingly Impossible

"But as for me, I will hope continually, and will praise You yet more and more." —Psalms 71:14

I WAS IN A CAR ACCIDENT ON SEPTEMBER 4, 2011. I HAD A fractured spine in several places, a broken ankle, a serious traumatic brain injury, a ruptured artery, and other injuries. The doctor did not think I would live, much less walk and talk again. I was airlifted to one hospital and remained in a coma for almost four weeks. When I regained consciousness, I was transported to another hospital.

My church had been praying for me, and I had at least two members come and pray with me every week. I overheard the doctors talking to my family about not getting their hopes up and that I probably would never be the same again. God's Word told me that He would heal me, and that is what I held on to. I was believing for 100 percent healing!

Today I still go to therapy, but I am walking, talking, driving short distances during the day and, at over fifty years old, am planning on going back to college for my masters in psychology. I believe He will make a way for me out of no way. I have already checked out a school and will be accepted. We serve a God of the impossible!

—Rosanne Powieski

Hope for Freedom from Fear

"For God has not given us a spirit of fear, but of power and of love and of a sound mind." —II Timothy 1:7 (NKJV)

THIS STORY BEGINS ON A WARM SPRING AFTERNOON. My buddies and I decided to take my friend's dad's new 1936 Chrysler sedan to go steal watermelons and "jump" hills on a dusty country road. We were trying to see how fast we could go on the open road. We managed to hit 85 to 95 miles per hour. As a front seat passenger, I noticed that at 92 mph, the steering wheel begin to rock.

The next thing I knew, we were airborne going end over end. The car landed on its side, slid up to a farmer's fence and stopped. We heard the sounds of broken glass, twisted metal and spinning wheels. Amazingly, all four of us were alive. I was the only one with a minor injury to my fingernails. They were driven back to the second joint. That was not too cool since I was a musician.

People gave their opinions as to how and why we all survived. Some said it was a miracle while others said we were lucky. I was fourteen years old when this happened and I was still trying to answer this question when I was twenty-one years old.

In the wintertime of 1950, I was in my sixth car wreck. I survived, but my buddy did not. I wasn't saved yet and carried guilt over my friend's death. I joined the Air Force and served four years during the Korean War. I was a camera tech on the RB36. I was honorably discharged. A little over a year after returning to my civilian environment, this time with a wife, one child and a new job, I started having panic attacks. I was checked by a doctor, who found me to be healthy; but I knew otherwise.

The panic attacks caused me to be stranded in my home with very little contact with the outside world. This continued for years and as a result, I lost my marriage and went through a divorce. I went to live with my parents, who were good enough to take me in.

Years later I was teaching music and promoting songwriters when I met the love of my life; my loving wife of twenty-six years. We began using Scripture to beat agoraphobia:

"For God has not given me the spirit of fear, but of power, love and a sound mind" (see II Timothy 1:7).

"There is no fear in love; but perfect love casts out fear, because fear has torment. But he who fears is not made perfect in love" (see I John 4:18).

In 1988, we took a car trip around the good old USA. I did most of the driving. I was taking prescribed medication at the time. We were believing for my healing and somewhere along the way during our trip, God really did heal me. I no longer needed my medication! When we returned home, I saw my psychiatrist and told him, "I guess with the meds and the Scripture I was healed." He looked at me and shook his head and uttered these words, "No! That was a miracle!" Jesus is the same yesterday, today and forever! If He could heal me, then he can surely heal you!

—Z'kharyah Pacos Mattoon

Hope in the One Who Heals

"But for you who fear My name the sun of righteousness will rise with healing in its wings..." —Malachi 4:2

OUR DAUGHTER, VICTORIA, HAD A RARE HEART DEFECT CALLED hypoplastic left heart syndrome (HLHS). She was born with only half of her heart, basically. The left ventricle never formed, thus leaving the right side to function alone. She needed three open-heart surgeries and a stent. Her first surgery was at six days old; the next surgery was at six months old; and the last surgery was when she was two and one half years old. It was devastating.

We believed Jesus healed her even though we had to go through all those surgeries. We believe she will never need another surgery again as we are standing on God's promises for total healing. *He who began a good work is able to complete it!* We prayed, believed and spoke God's Word daily.

Our daughter has defied all odds! Many other children born with HLHS have Down syndrome or other health problems because of their heart defect and the surgeries they have to undergo. Victoria is above and beyond healthy! If God can heal an infant's heart, then there is nothing too difficult for Him!

—*Dawn Curiale*

Hope for Promotion

"For not from the east nor the west nor from the south come promotion and lifting up. But God is the Judge! He puts down one and lifts up another." —Psalms 75:6-7 (AMP)

I STOOD AT THE BOARD LOOKING TO SEE WHO HAD GOTTEN THE promotion, the job I wanted so very much, and John was standing next to me. I felt hurt when I saw it wasn't me. Well, I knew it wasn't me already because I would have been called into the office, received my congratulations, and signed my papers accepting the position and the salary. To my dismay, the person selected had only been working in the office for six months.

While I was standing there, John said, "Now that's a shame! You should file a grievance. That should have been your job. You've been here longer than he has!" To give you a little background about the job, it was a technical management position, and I could not approach the union because it wasn't a union job. All I could do was file a grievance, stating they had discriminated against me by giving it to Jim, a white male.

I told John, "He is probably more qualified than I am. But do you know what? This just means that God has something much better and more exciting for me. I'll check into it, but I'll just wait and see what God has in store!" At that point, I could feel the butterflies in my stomach and joy bubbled up inside because I knew if not this, then there had to be something better that He had for me to do.

I scheduled the appointment with the selecting official and this is what I was told: "I am so sorry, but Jim was better qualified because he brought the experience with him from the outside."

All I could say was, "OK!" I stood up, smiled, shook his hand and left the office. I was still so excited that I was about to burst.

Shortly after that, I was promoted to another technical management position in another office. As I was leaving, I spoke to my general manager and asked him if I didn't like my new position could I come back? He teasingly replied, "Sure, but you'll have to start at the bottom again!"

I said, "No! I think when I come back I'll come back in your position as the general manager." We both laughed...but I was speaking in faith. A general manager was considered an executive of the company. The technical management positions reported to the supervisors, who reported to branch managers, who then reported to the general managers. The general manager's position also came along with certain perks!

Well, it took me all of eight years from the day I was hired before I sat in that general manager's chair, in my office looking around. I had made it! I still had the butterflies and all of the excitement I had whenever I been promoted over time. The first thing I said was, "Thank You, Lord! I knew You had something better for me."

Of course, when I was awarded this job, my prior general manager called me and said, "I can't believe you actually did it!"

I responded, "It is by faith that I am here. I knew God had something in store, but I never imagined this!"

I retired in 2009. Jim retired in 2008 in the same job that I wanted so long ago. I am so grateful that I did not file that grievance. I have the experience to be able to say, "Let God be God! He knows what His plan is for you!"

—Jeannie Thomas

Hope for Eternal Life

*"...We are of good courage, I say, and prefer rather to be absent
from the body and to be at home with the Lord."*
—II Corinthians 5:8

IN 1979, I FOUND MYSELF THE SINGLE MOM OF THREE (two boys and a girl), and joining a new church. I worked full time and supported us with my salary alone. My daughter became seriously ill, and after many tests, the doctors determined she needed a liver transplant. My new church had recently received funds from a donor to set up a catastrophic fund to be used for anyone who, through no fault of their own, was faced with financial debts above and beyond what could be afforded.

The Lord provided the rent on my apartment and airline tickets to Denver, Colorado, where we stayed for three and a half months. My employer gave me the time off with no pay, but my benefits continued. As I prayed daily for my sons and my daughter, the devotional, *Streams in the Desert,* was a great source of comfort to me. God foreknew my circumstances and provided before I ever called out to Him.

My daughter was fifteen, and my youngest son, who was ten years old, stayed with a family in the church while I was in Denver. My oldest son was in junior college in Pennsylvania. My daughter received the transplant and did well enough for us to come home for Thanksgiving. The team of doctors who tended to my daughter left Denver and relocated to Pittsburgh, which was a blessing because it was closer to where I lived in New Jersey. There was an airline price war going on at the time and I was able to fly to Pittsburgh for $39.

My daughter suffered rejection and needed another transplant. All in all, she had three transplants. The Lord gave us three and a half more years with her. While in Pittsburgh, I met a Christian mom whose seventeen-month-old baby had heart problems since birth. My daughter was seventeen at the time. One morning I got up from the couch I slept on in the lobby of the hospital and saw my friend crying. I got up and walked over to her. I felt the compassion of the Lord rise up in me and I knelt down by her and held her, and we cried together. Her daughter had just died.

Not more than twenty-four hours later, my own daughter passed away. I had a dream of a white casket with mauve interior, and her body ascending to heaven. I want you to know that Psalms 23 is accurate: *"Though I walk through the valley of the shadow of death, I will fear no evil: for thou art with me..."* (KJV). There is no shadow without light, and Jesus is the Light of the World.

My daughter had rededicated her life to Christ at a Christian camp the summer before she became ill. She was an incredible witness to so many. I received hundreds of letters from all over the country and a special one from the hospital administrator. Suffice it to say, no matter what you are faced with, God is able! He is our Deliverer! Death is not the worst fate for a Christian. I know I shall see her again!

—*Charlotte Weaver Koerner*

Hope in the One Who Orders Our Steps

"The steps of a man are established by the Lord, and He delights in his way." —Psalms 37:23

HAVE BEEN SERVING IN RUSSIA THE PAST FIVE YEARS with a missionary organization that conducts medical expeditions, sharing God's love with the "forgotten" Russian people who live in remote parts of Russia. Carrying multiple ministry responsibilities with an intense schedule for over a year, I was physically exhausted and felt I needed a break. A vacation to Spain's sunny coast seemed a viable option. It was only four hours away and the airfare was reasonable, at least compared to flying from the U.S. Last spring, I booked accommodations for two weeks so for two months I looked forward to my upcoming trip and "getting away."

The big day came! I arrived at the municipal airport and stood in the line leading to the ticket counter. The security person took my passport and my new Temporary Residency Permit. After looking it over, she declared that I didn't have the proper documentation. She said I could not board the airplane! Apparently, I also needed an exit visa to leave the country. This was news to me! When I applied for the Residency Permit, I made sure all my bases were covered. Nothing was said to me about an exit visa! I called one of our staff to speak with the security person over the phone since I knew only a few basic phrases of the local language like, "Where is the Metro?"

After a lengthy discussion and calls to the consulate, I had to face the fact that I wasn't going anywhere that day or the next. As I stood there in the airport deciding what to do next, I had this overpowering sensation of God's love. These words rose up out of my spirit: "God loves me so much, He didn't want me to go!" Believe me, this was not a "Pollyanna, everything-is-rosy" attitude on my part. I returned home very disappointed, yet trusting that God was in control.

A week later, I happened to click on a European Internet news site that I had never visited before. Flashing across the screen at that moment was a news headline about a fire that was spreading over a coastal town in Spain; the very town I had planned to visit at the very time I would have been there!

So often when we come up against barriers or run into adverse circumstances, we blame our adversary, the devil. We overlook God's great love, failing to trust that, ultimately, *His ways are higher than our ways* (see Isaiah 55:9).

There is more to the story! Two months later, I got word that my daughter, Lisa, was in an Oregon Hospital ICU, unconscious and in critical condition with meningitis, encephalitis, a bacterial infection and high blood sugar levels. Not planning to go to the U.S. any time soon, I hadn't yet applied for the exit visa. When I learned of my daughter's illness, I immediately looked into getting the visa and was told it would take three weeks! Through the persuasive gifts of a dear local doctor who went with me to the immigration office, I was issued the permit on that very day. I was in Oregon the next day at my daughter's hospital bedside! Praise God! If I hadn't had that problem at the airport when I tried to go to Spain, I wouldn't have known about the exit permit. I would have shown up at the airport ready to board a plane to see my daughter, and been refused!

By the way, Lisa's doctor is amazed at her recovery. She had no lasting effects from being unconscious for three days, except for her irregular blood sugar levels. I am praying the diabetes is abated and all of her bodily systems are reset to normal as God has intended them to be! Best of all, she knows Jesus saved her life for a purpose! She will fulfill her destiny! Amen, and to God be the glory!

—*Pat M.*

Hope for a Change of Heart

"God's servant must not be argumentative, but a gentle listener and a teacher who keeps cool, working firmly but patiently with those who refuse to obey. You never know how or when God might sober them up with a change of heart and a turning to the truth, enabling them to escape the Devil's trap, where they are caught...forced to run his errands."
—II Timothy 2:24-26 (The Message)

WHEN I WAS IN HIGH SCHOOL, I WAS A VERY GOOD ATHLETE. In my senior year, I was voted Athlete of the Syosset High School and made the all-county baseball team. I never did drugs as I prepared myself to play professional baseball. That was all I could think about. I was given a full scholarship to Florida to play ball, but I tore the ligaments in my left arm and could never pitch again. I had to come home and push concrete and dig holes with the construction company my father worked with.

I hated my life, so I found a solution. I turned to doing drugs. I did any drug I could get my hands on. I was arrested many times for cocaine possession and DWIs. My mind was on one thing—doing drugs. Year after year, I went to work, drank a little and then went on a mission to buy drugs. As the years went by, I began to regret never getting married and having a family of my own. I did not care if I lived or if I died. I was bound and depressed. I spent many years doing outpatient therapy, inpatient therapy and went to Catholic charities. I was also on probation for years. Nothing seemed to work or to help me.

My parents never gave up on me and kept praying for me. My father and mother helped me buy a house, and we started a construction business together. I could never live in the house because of my drug problem, so I rented it out. One day, two nice people came to rent the house and invited me to their church to see a show. I went to church with them and after the service I went up and prayed the salvation prayer. I thought I meant it, but the next four years were worse than ever.

I lost my company; I lost my house; I lost my car; and I lost my battle against drugs. As fast as my father would buy a tool for the company, I would turn around and sell it to get the next drug. I broke my parents' hearts. My life was a living nightmare. I knew I was never going to have my own family, and I knew I had failed in life. I had failed at being a son to my father.

Then I managed to quit drinking for two months. I had done that before, but it never took. I always went back. I went to church and confessed my sin. I spoke it with my mouth and meant it with my heart. Early in the morning, around 12:30 A.M., God delivered me from the unholy spirit that had kept me bound all those years. I woke my father and mother and told them what happened. God somehow revealed to me that if I ever went back to living the way I had up to that point, that spirit would be there waiting for me. From that moment on, faith was birthed in me.

After a few years, I ran into some old friends who invited me to their church. I went and for the first time really heard the Word of God. I knew then that with the help of Jesus, I could rebuild my life. It has been seven years now and God has restored my mother and father's love. I am not married and still don't have children, but I no longer feel badly about myself. The people of God are my family, and I now have a new mission—to tell world that Jesus loves them, and all He has done for me!

God has given me the gift of eternal life. I thank God for delivering me, saving me and for restoring my life. I will, with the help of the Holy Spirit, serve Jesus with every breath until the day I die. Without Him, I am nothing!

—*Holden Chandler*

Hope When All Seems Lost

"For what does it profit a man to gain the whole world, and forfeit his life [in the eternal kingdom of God]?"
—Mark 8:36 (AMP)

HAD IT ALL. I WAS SUCCESSFUL BEYOND MY DREAMS. I am American, but I worked in Europe and Asia for almost twenty years in about a half dozen countries. I eventually met my "soul mate" while I was living in Malta. Malta was where the apostle Paul was shipwrecked. We got married and had two sons while living there.

I was raised a Catholic, and Malta had a large Catholic population. I faithfully went to church with my family, but did not have a personal relationship with Christ.

I had achieved the American dream. I had a successful career, a beautiful wife and two incredible sons. We owned a beautiful house in Florida, one in Malta, and others in Croatia, Hungry, Poland and Greece; to name a few of the places where we lived and worked.

We decided to come back to Florida to raise the boys. My success went to my head, and I became more and more enticed by the riches of the world. Yes, I still went to church, but it was mainly for appearances and to set an example for my young sons.

I became involved in a business "opportunity" that turned out to be a money-laundering operation. I knew what I was doing, but I didn't really think what we were doing was illegal. It would not have been in Europe, but things are different in the U.S. I was found guilty and went to federal prison for two years. During my incarceration, my "dream" marriage to my soul mate turned sour. My wife divorced me while in prison, and remarried a friend of ours. I was devastated.

I lost my wife, my sons, my reputation, my money...I lost everything! But it was while I was incarcerated that I found freedom and liberty in Christ Jesus!

I met a man named Howard Chewning who taught a small group of men in prison about the Bible. He mentored me diligently. Many thought I had found "prison religion" but it was much more than that. I enrolled in a correspondence Bible study course and graduated after three years. I began my studies while in prison and continued on for a year after my release.

Howard was incarcerated for almost twelve years. He led many men to Christ during that time, and he still does in Jacksonville, Florida. He was released almost two years ago, and I was released almost seven years ago.

I continue to read and study the Bible every morning to get my day moving in the "right" direction. The true riches of this world are found only in Christ Jesus!

—Jay Stoelting

Against All Odds, Hope in God

"And a woman who had had a hemorrhage for twelve years, and had endured much at the hands of many physicians, and had spent all that she had and was not helped at all, but rather had grown worse, after hearing about Jesus, came up in the crowd behind Him, and touched His cloak. For she thought, 'If I just touch His garments, I will get well.' Immediately the flow of her blood was dried up; and she felt in her body that she was healed of her affliction." —Mark 5:25-29

I WOKE UP ONE DAY IN 2009 TO SEVERE ABDOMINAL PAIN. I was rushed to the hospital. While there they gave me blood thinners for what they say was a blood clot in my left kidney, which the doctors gave up as lost. I was released from the hospital and in the middle of the night a few evenings later, I started hemorrhaging to death from my intestines. I got up to get help, but fell into a closet making a loud noise which caused my children to wake up. They immediately called 911. The ambulance took me to the hospital emergency room where the doctor told my family that I would not survive. Around midnight, the chief radiology surgeon from a neighboring hospital made an unscheduled visit. He took my hand, and somewhere between consciousness and unconsciousness, he told me that he was there to help me.

I underwent surgery where he went through a vein in my leg with computer imaging and repaired the ruptured artery. I was awake for this procedure because I was too weak to be sedated. I was taken to intensive care where my entire family filed in one by one. My ex-husband, who had abandoned me years before, also came to visit me. I was able to make peace with him and offered him forgiveness and apologized for anything I ever did to hurt him.

Four hours later, I was sitting up and talking to a rheumatologist who informed me that I had a rare autoimmune disease, which made my blood clot, then bleed. For the next several months, I received chemotherapy and massive steroids. My children brought me my CD player with Pastor Mark Chironna's CD on the woman with the issue of blood. In his teaching, he said it was my time to get up and cited the woman with the issue of blood. He said to reach out and touch Jesus. I listened to this CD over and over again, and chose life.

I never saw the doctor who performed my surgery after that night in the emergency room. The nurses and doctor who were treating me told me it was a miracle he was there. I was tested again months later, and every evidence of my abdominal trauma has disappeared, except for the metal clip where the artery was repaired. My left kidney, which the doctor said would never function again, is fully functioning and healthy. I have also been released from the care of the rheumatologist because I no longer have any evidence of an autoimmune disease.

It was a long road to recovery, but I soaked in the Word and believed that if God could heal the woman with the issue of blood over 2,000 years ago, He could heal me, too!

—K.

Hope in the God Who Works Miracles

"He sent His word and healed them..." —Psalms 107:20

ABOUT TWENTY-FOUR YEARS AGO, I WENT TO THE BEST doctors I could find in order to have my gallbladder removed because of stomach problems. I thought it would be a routine surgery. I underwent the procedure and returned home a few weeks later. As I was going through recovery at home, complications set in.

I had yellow jaundice and internal bleeding. I had a second operation and was in my room after surgery when all of a sudden, I passed out and the machine flatlined. The best way to describe what I was feeling is to say I felt like I was fainting within myself. My mother was with me, and before I went out, I saw two men standing beside her. I thought it was my brother and cousin. She later told me they were not there. I believe God had angels standing beside her.

My mother was a praying woman who believed in the power of God. I thought I was in heaven when I came back around because I heard talking, but it was the doctors hooking me up to a breathing machine. I thought no one cared about me at the time, but God had many people praying for me, including ministers; praying Christians; my insurance man, Mr. Broher; and even hospital workers.

I was in intensive care for twenty-two days hooked up to a breathing machine and a heart monitor. The doctors had done all they could do for me in the natural, and both of them got on their knees and prayed for me along with my mom. My family kept praying for me.

I got a little better and was assigned to a private room. One day the nurse sat me up in a chair. I was so weak I could not even hold a fork in my hands or move on my own. I remember my mom speaking these words: "God, I am looking for a miracle today!" When she spoke those words, God touched me. I felt that touch begin in my toes, move through my feet, up my legs and into my hips, and I got out of that chair! God moved in me that very day! That was the first miracle! The nurses knew I could not move on my own and their eyes got really big when they saw me get up!

I lay in bed while the nurse checked me out. A cloud entered the room and I heard God say, "I will give you everything back!"

I thank God for a praying mom! She went home to be with the Lord in 2006, and I miss her dearly. She told me to always have faith in God, and she diligently prayed for all nine of her children. She was a prayer warrior, and when she spoke in faith, God showed up and did the rest! I will never forget how God saved my life back in 1989 to 1990 after a three-month hospital stay. He is a healing God!

—*Mable Jones*

Hope for a Life of Freedom

"So now, I will break his yoke bar from upon you, and I will tear off your shackles." —Nahum 1:13

I REMEMBER GROWING UP IN A STRICT CATHOLIC HOME. I was very sheltered and like many young girls, I dreamed of getting married and having children one day. However, when I left home and went to university, I became involved in a lesbian relationship. What I thought would bring me happiness, brought me shame, grief and turmoil. Even though I felt my behavior was wrong, I also felt like I was trapped in the lifestyle that I had chosen; so I resigned myself to homosexuality. Eventually, the internal turmoil became unbearable and, with sheer determination, I put a stop to my behavior.

As time passed, I learned about the love of Jesus Christ and became a born-again Christian. I began attending a church where I felt loved and a sense of belonging. Six years into my Christian walk, I allowed myself to become involved in a homosexual relationship within the church. I had stopped this behavior before, and now I was repeating old patterns of behavior with people who claimed to be children of God, as I did. Once again, I became overwhelmed with pain, guilt, shame and self-condemnation. I did not believe that this was what God wanted for my life. I felt judged and persecuted by some of the church people who I thought loved me. I felt hopeless and alone. The stress of the situation resulted in my hospitalization because of a nervous breakdown. I felt life my life was over. The situation brought me to a place of isolation. There was no one for me to turn to but God—only I wanted to run away from Him, the people who hurt me, and the church where I met my Savior.

Instead, I chose to stay and challenge God. I cried out to Him, "If You are really true and You really love me, then You have to show me that You are real! I want to live a life of freedom, victory, and the abundant life that You promise in Your Word!"

I began a fresh, new and amazing journey with God. He poured out His love and His amazing grace and opened my heart to experience His unconditional love, acceptance and deep inner healing. It was this experience that led me to the pathway that God had chosen for me.

Several years later, I married a loving and caring man. His first priority was to love God. His second priority was to love me, knowing all my past, faults and weaknesses. His love for me is an expression of God's great love for me.

I was very happy that my former life had passed, and I was now living the life I dreamed of as a young girl; or so I thought. Sometime after our marriage, my husband and I decided to start a family. I was in my thirties, so I went to my family doctor to do a series of tests in order to prepare myself for childbirth. Her tests revealed that I was unable to get pregnant, so she referred us to a fertility specialist. My body did not have the ability to produce eggs, and the fact that I was very close to menopause did not help. The specialist explained that the only way I could get pregnant was if I had an egg donor. I was devastated and felt as if God was punishing me for my past behavior; but something inside of me could not believe that this could be true of the loving heavenly Father I had come to know.

Shortly after the specialist's diagnosis, I became pregnant. We were overjoyed; unfortunately, six weeks into the pregnancy, I miscarried. We were emotionally distraught. Once again, I felt as though God was punishing me. But inside I knew this was a lie, so we didn't give up. I did the only thing I knew how to do; I went to God's Word. I looked up every scripture about barrenness and every scripture about women who had children. I looked up every promise about who God is and every promise that broke every curse. I began to believe with my husband, and we asked God to create just one healthy egg.

We pleaded with Him and stood upon His promises, and after three years, He answered.

Although the specialist said my body was unable to produce eggs, I knew I served a God who is able. He brought forth a beautiful baby girl and sixteen months later, an amazing, healthy baby boy.

My husband and I are blessed. Our family continues to serve God and fellowship at the same church that God had originally brought us to, enjoying the freedom of His amazing love.

—Anonymous

Hope for a Savior

"...And thou shalt know that I the Lord am thy Savior and thy Redeemer, the mighty One of Jacob." —Isaiah 60:16 (KJV)

As a dying Muslim at the age of thirty-three, the Lord saved me, healed me and delivered me. The doctors had given up hope that my broken life could ever be mended. They put me on Prozac and sleeping pills to help me cope with my broken heart and the oppression on my mind. Nothing they did to try and help me cured my problems.

Then I met Jesus, my Savior and Redeemer! He healed my broken heart and restored my mind...awesome God that He is! He truly is the Resurrection and the Life! When no one or nothing else could help and deliver me, He did!

—Gloria Dean

Hope to Become a Joyful Mother

"He maketh the barren woman to keep house, and to be a joyful mother of children. Praise ye the Lord." —Psalms 113:9 (KJV)

MY STORY IS NOT RECENT, BUT I BELIEVE THAT IT MAY BE an encouragement to women who are believing God for the ability to conceive a child. In January of 1974, three doctors confirmed that I would likely never conceive a child because of a condition called endometriosis. The walls of my uterus were in a constant state of tearing down.

On the day I received that report, I felt stunned because I was not expecting to hear such news. I recall stepping out of the doctor's office that day into a bright and sunny day proclaiming that they didn't have the final say and that God is the giver of life. As I drove home, I couldn't wipe the smile off my face because it felt like my faith in God went into overdrive just knowing that God's Word said something different about my life than the report of the doctors.

By March of 1974, I was back in the doctor's office hemorrhaging profusely. He gave me a shot of something (I don't recall what) and in a day or so, the hemorrhaging completely stopped. I got through the entire summer without any problems, still holding fast to God's Word. I chose life no matter what.

I kept my follow-up appointment in October of 1974. After a thorough examination, the doctor came into the room with a puzzled look on his face and said, "Betty, you are no longer infertile, and you are four to six weeks pregnant."

I was overjoyed! I was so thankful I did not receive the initial report of the doctors. The doctor confirmed what the Lord had shown me in a dream one month before the appointment: that I was indeed pregnant! All that kept resounding in my spirit as I left the doctor's office that day was, "Whose report will you believe?"

My beautiful daughter was born on June 17, 1975. God is able, and I am living proof!

—Betty White

Hope for Our Offspring

"Can a woman forget her nursing child and have no compassion on the son of her womb? Even these may forget, but I will not forget you. Behold, I have inscribed you on the palms of My hands...." —Isaiah 49:15-16

M Y YOUNGER SON, JEREMY, WAS DIAGNOSED IN 1998 with Asperger's Syndrome (on the autism spectrum). He was born on October 6, 1994, and is now eighteen years old.

My husband, Ellis, and I have been praying, fasting and sowing seeds toward the complete healing of Jeremy. For me, I was expecting God to just take away the autism and make him "perfect." However, that was not God's plan. Over the years, we have seen positive changes in Jeremy. In the past, we had to restrict his exposure to crowded environments. He even graduated early from a special education school in June 2012 and then was suspended from a center for special needs people after attending for one month because he was having frequent episodes of tantrums. He was also becoming very violent at home, breaking things. He would rarely ever smile. Because of the stress of having to deal with all of this, I felt as though 2012 was the worst year of my life.

Furthermore, for many years Jeremy's blood pressure was spiking beyond 140 over 90, and this became an increasing concern. His weight was over 230 pounds and he was considered borderline obese. He is six feet tall.

Things became even more stressful when we learned that our older son, who is twenty-one years old, had gotten his fiancée pregnant in August of that year.

My husband and I began to earnestly seek the Lord as we felt our family was being hit from every angle. As the year drew to a close, we saw things begin to turn around for our family. Our son got married to his fiancée on December 15, 2012, and their daughter is expected to arrive on March 27, 2013. We have embraced their union and have been supporting them and showing them the love of God.

As for our son Jeremy, his blood pressure has come down to 119 over 71, and his weight has dropped to 176 pounds. We did not have to put him on a strict diet. We just ensured that he ate at reasonable intervals. He is now at home, and we are in the process of developing a program to work with him. His joy is now restored. His ability to grasp things continues to improve. He is really working on having conversations with us. This is difficult for him, but I can see that he is really making an effort. He got water baptized a week after he turned eighteen in October 2012, and he is now able to be in church for the entire service. He loves to worship God!

I believe that as others have watched us go through struggles with our children and have seen God intervene on our behalf, it has given them strength and encouragement that they too can face battles and win! God is able to do abundantly above and beyond all that we could ever dream!

—Camele Burke

Hope for a Joyful Heart

"Then the virgin will rejoice in the dance, and the young men and the old, together, for I will turn their mourning into joy and will comfort them and give them joy for their sorrow."
—Jeremiah 31:13

GREW UP AS THE YOUNGEST AND ONLY GIRL WITH FOUR older brothers in a wealthy family. My dad owned his own oil and gas company, and my mom stayed home.

We all went to Catholic school, which was very strict, although at home, we really didn't have any boundaries. However, my brothers got to go and do things I could not, simply because I was a girl.

My mom was part Hispanic and never knew her dad, so she wrestled with rejection issues. My dad was a functioning alcoholic, because he was smart.

I always felt like an orphan. Everyone in my household did their own thing. Some days I never talked to anyone. I went to school, went to track, went to gymnastics, came home, ate by myself, did my homework, went to bed, and woke up the next morning to repeat the same thing, day after day.

I didn't seem to fit in at school, either. I just felt different and always struggled to make C's. This was difficult for me because my brothers were very good students and very popular.

In the ninth grade, I became desperately depressed. I hated life. I started starving myself. I guess I was seeking attention or maybe just control over something in my life. I did get attention. Everyone at school knew me as the girl with anorexia.

My track coach called my mom and told her to take me to the doctor, and he kicked me off the team. I threw my uniform at him and said he could have it, but he couldn't stop me from running. So, I continued running, and starving.

Finally, when I realized it was affecting my brain and the way I thought, and that it didn't really make me any better than anyone else, I started eating. I remember the day God took anorexia away from me. I didn't want to stop being that way, but God had a plan for my life.

I got better and went away to Kansas to college where I started going to a Bible study on campus. There I met Jesus as my personal Lord and Savior.

Now I walk with Him in the joy of the Lord, have a purpose to my life and take care of myself. I am a personal trainer and am thinking about getting my nutrition degree. God is opening His plan for my life from day to day!

—Anne

Hope for Him to Complete What He Has Begun

"Being confident of this very thing, that he which hath begun a good work in you will perform it until the day of Jesus Christ...."
—Philippians 1:6 (KJV)

MY STORY IS A WORK IN PROGRESS AS GOD IS STILL MOVING in my life, and I'm looking forward to each day with Him. About six years ago, after making a 911 call, I left my abusive husband. It was the scariest thing I ever had to do, but for the sake of our young daughter, I had to leave. I knew I could not put my trust in the family court system (which needs an overhaul), so I learned to put my trust in the faithfulness of God. He has not left my daughter or me alone; He is ever present!

God led me to a Word of Faith church, and this is where my healing began. My daughter still has overnight visitations with my ex, her dad. He is verbally abusive to her, but there is not enough evidence for the courts to keep her from him. He uses our daughter to get back at me for leaving. There is nothing I can do legally, so I've learned to cast this care on Him. I am believing that God will grant me wisdom to move this mountain.

It has been a long journey, and I am still learning to hear His voice. Even though I have not seen God move things in a more positive direction for my daughter, I do know this: I no longer believe that God hates me, that I am a mistake and that I deserved all the beatings and tongue-lashings I received. It took me years to accept God's love. Years of abuse convinced me that I was worthless and unwanted by God.

But thanks be to God and the Holy Spirit for leading me in the Scriptures and to an incredible church where I am receiving teachings that have transformed my life. Truth is healing my heart!

—Samara Schmidt

Hope for the Future

"'For I know the plans that I have for you,' declares the Lord, 'plans for welfare and not for calamity to give you a future and a hope.'" —Jeremiah 29:11

I AM AN ISLAND GIRL, AND I COME FROM THE BEAUTIFUL archipelago of The Bahamas. I was born as the last of three girls. Both of my parents had me in the midst of separating and divorcing from previous relationships. I was the fruit of their unwed union.

I grew up in a home where there was a lot of emotional baggage to work through. In a nutshell, there were times when I felt I was the reason for my parents' unhappiness. Often when they argued, I felt rejected and unaccepted.

I made a decision to become a Christian at a young age in search of something I could not identify at the time. I understand now it was a sense of acceptance. For many years on my Christian walk, I believed that holiness and goodness were connected to perfection (the absence of making mistakes), piety and reservedness. This was how I lived most of my Christian life while attending Christian school.

I was very isolated emotionally, suffering with much fear and anxiety because I took on the highs and lows of my parents' problems. I acted older than I actually was and struggled with a deep sense of loneliness.

God was always watching over me as I grew up, although I didn't always feel Him. After my high school years and into my time in college, I began to cry out for more and more freedom in my soul and spirit. You see what people saw on the outside was not actually who I was on the inside. I had imprisoned myself. My pious appearance was a façade, a mask I worked on to protect myself. I was relying on my own strength instead of my relationship with God.

About relationship...Christianity for me spelt out religion and rules, not relationship. My mind was a far cry away from understanding what grace was. To say the least, I needed a revamp of my view of God, where I didn't identify Him as my parents.

I struggled for a long time with unforgiveness toward my parents—for things they did and didn't do. Life had its ups, downs, mistakes and misunderstandings. I had to forgive them for being human. Eventually I did and I still ask the Lord to help me to remember that I have already forgiven, and to let go.

My lifelong dream was to one day become an attorney and more specifically, an advocate. I devoted my energies in school to studying to one day become what I dreamed.

That lifelong dream did come to pass, and it was a joyous time for me. However, shortly after my call to the Bar, some unexpected events occurred. About a week after my call, I was released from my job as a part-time student. With no work in sight and a dream delayed, I didn't know what my next step should have been. While looking for work, three weeks after my call, early one morning, someone broke into my home and raped me. To this day, I don't know who the person was. I later discovered that he was stalking me, and that he was a serial rapist.

Devastated and disillusioned, I left my beautiful island nation and came to Orlando, Florida and stayed with a girlfriend to begin my healing and recovery process. Three weeks later, I moved to Miami and lived with my sister and brother-in-law for one year and one month before returning home. In that time, I was engaged in deep healing and restorative work. The process was arduous. There was nothing easy or pain-free... but God!

I write here and ask the simple, obvious question: Where was God in the midst of it all? Where was God when I felt alone as a little girl? Where was God when I couldn't fix my parents' relationship and problems? Where was God when I felt un-acceptable and rejected? Where was God when I lost my job? Where was God when I was raped?

When I headed to college, away from home for the first time, the Holy Spirit led me to read this passage in the Bible. The passage was Jeremiah 29. I didn't know what the significance of the chapter was, so I just read it. I paid no close attention to it at the time, but while struggling in college, the Lord reminded me of that chapter and showed me the verse that would be a lifelong companion for me, and a comfort in my dark days ahead. Jeremiah 29:11 reads, *"For I know the plans that I have for you..."*

Where was God? He was right there.

When I struggled with fear and loneliness, and sometimes still do, I'm reminded of Scripture passages such as *"Be still and know that I am God," "Fear not, it is I," "Don't be afraid, I will be with you"* and *"I will never leave you nor forsake you."* (See Psalms 46:10; Matthew 14:27; Isaiah 43:1-2; Hebrews 13:5.)

Where was God? He was right there.

And when I was raped, I heard the Holy Spirit say to me, *"You shall live and not die and declare the works of the Lord,"* and, *"All things work together for good to those who love God and are called according to His purpose"* (see Psalms 118:17; Romans 8:28). The Holy Spirit whispered that sweet Sunday school song in my spirit: "Yes, Jesus loves me!"

Where was God? He was right there.

And...

Where is God now? He is right here with me, because I'm sharing this story...and with you, because you're reading it. What an awesome God I serve!

—Annie-Laurie

Hope Against All Odds

"The fundamental fact of existence is that this trust in God, this faith, is the firm foundation under everything that makes life worth living. It's our handle on what we can't see..."
—Hebrews 11:1 (The Message)

MY STORY BEGAN THIRTY-FIVE YEARS AGO WHEN THE doctor told me I was pregnant. That was my first miracle because my uterus was filled with tumors. The doctor then proceeded to tell me that I would not be able to successfully carry the baby to full term, but I did!

The doctor said my only recourse was to have an abortion because of my physical challenges, but I refused! My baby girl was about to be born, but the doctor said because of other complications, my baby would not make it through the delivery, but she did!

Over the next seven years, my little girl went through many near-death experiences and we saw miracle after miracle, year after year. And she made it without the doctors' help.

She is now thirty-four years old with four children of her own and is absolutely healthy! She is a walking miracle! I have always believed in hope against hope and calling those things that are not as though they are and have seen God move on Kim's behalf all through her life!

We serve a God who is faithful to His Word and will bring victory every time!

—Linda Moore

Hope That He Is in Absolute Control

"And we know that God causes all things to work together for good to those who love God, to those who are called according to His purpose." —Romans 8:28

ON THIS PARTICULAR CRISP OCTOBER MORNING AROUND 7:00 A.M., I had just gotten off work from my third shift job at a local hotel in downtown Orlando, where I work as a night auditor. I drove to church and got an hour-long nap in my car before going inside and changing out of my uniform into my Sunday clothes.

I sang in the two morning services, as I am on the praise and worship team. After the second service, once the praise and worship was over, I walked to my car to head home and finally get some rest. A fellow church member came up to me and asked me if I could give her a ride to the local mall. I had seen her several times before walking to and from church and had given her rides to the bus stop in the past, so I was familiar with her situation and knew she was going through a rough time. Though I was tired, I was happy to bless her with a ride.

I drove her to the mall and headed home. It began to rain. It was not a downpour, but just enough to make the roads slick. I reached my exit off Interstate 4 and was two miles away from my home. Suddenly, my car began to hydroplane, and I lost control of my car. I veered over to the center lane, but quickly regained control of my car and pulled back into the right lane where I had been driving. I then felt something hit my car from behind, which caused my car to go into a 360-degree spin. My car smashed into the guardrail and veered off the road. It was as if everything began to occur in slow motion. I could see a large grassy plot of land in front of me. All I could do was await the inevitable impact. I crashed and totaled my car.

As it turned out, another member of our church drove the car that hit me from behind. I could see the other driver was now out of her car surveying the damage. She came over to my door to make sure I was all right. By this time, other good Samaritans had also come to my car to check on me. My back and leg were throbbing, and everyone advised me to wait in the car until help arrived.

The fire department and paramedics came and helped to remove me from the car. The impact of the crash caused my spinal cord to shift and slant like the Leaning Tower of Pisa, which explained why my back was in such pain. I had to undergo physical therapy for the next year. I am thankful we serve a healing God who has restored me completely!

Eleven months later, I was leaving church after a late rehearsal with the praise team. Since my car had been totaled in the accident the year before, I used the check from the insurance company and bought an old used Chrysler Sebring, which seemed huge in comparison to my previous Toyota Yaris. I was driving down Markham Woods Road, which is a road known for having a great deal of wild life. All of a sudden, a huge black bear darted in front of my car. I hit the bear before I even realized what happened. The bear ran back into the woods. I feared the bear might attack me if I got out of my car, so I thought it was wiser for me to drive straight home.

When I got there, I surveyed the damage along with my family. There were two huge dents on the front of the car where the bear hit the hood. I was incredibly frightened and was still shaking. I told my family that I was no longer going to drive. Between the car accident that previous October and this run-in with the bear, I decided I should just stay off the road. I was too afraid to get behind the wheel ever again. My dad wouldn't allow that to happen. He said, "You're looking at this the wrong way. That accident in October was a blessing in disguise. You were blessed with the means to help a fellow church member who didn't have what you had. You gave her a ride to the mall and afterwards got into an accident, but that accident was a blessing in disguise. If you hadn't had that accident, you would still be driving that small Yaris. If you had been driving that smaller car and hit that bear, given the damage on your car, you might not be here right now."

In that moment, God reminded me that He knows the plans He has for me. He took those frightening accidents to remind me that He dispatches His ministering angels around me day and night. If not for Him, I would not have survived. I am thankful that God was able to show me firsthand that the same event that initially seemed devastating ended up being a blessing in disguise. I am so thankful for God's hand of protection over my life, and that His blessings are not for us alone, but to be shared with others. I have a peace in knowing that even in my darkest, scariest hour, my God is still in control.

—Hope Victoria Walton Charles

Hope to Find His Love

"How blessed is God! And what a blessing he is! He's the Father of our Master, Jesus Christ, and takes us to the high places of blessing in Him. Long before he laid down earth's foundations, he had us in mind, had settled on us as the focus of his love, to be made whole and holy by his love. Long, long ago he decided to adopt us into his family through Jesus Christ. (What pleasure he took in planning this!) He wanted us to enter into the celebration of His lavish gift-giving by the hand of his beloved Son." —Ephesians 1:3-6 (The Message)

FORTY YEARS WENT BY BEFORE I "GOT IT." I'M A MOM with two children, now eight and twelve and a half years old. I grew up in a pastor's home. Church was our life. We had church Sunday mornings at 10:00 A.M. and Sunday evenings at 7:00 P.M. We had communion service Wednesday evenings, Bible study on Friday evenings, and youth group on Saturday evenings. I believed that my parents were very strict when I was growing up, but it turns out they were just very angry. We sat in the front pew with Mom and dared not turn around until we were dismissed for Sunday school.

Years and years went by with the same church schedule. Aside from church, we were not allowed to go anywhere. There was no grade-nine graduation for me. My friends were not allowed to come over my house, and we definitely were not allowed to go over their houses. We were not permitted to go to the movies or play cards, and makeup was forbidden. We were told that all of that was "of the devil." How I longed for freedom!

By the age of twenty-one, I was married, but by the very next day after my wedding, I knew I had made a mistake and was divorced that same year. I started partying with friends, which was something I was not very familiar with, but I certainly grew to enjoy it. That became my life for the next ten years. I jumped from relationship to relationship with no concern or care for myself. Within this ten-year period, I had my daughter. I was twenty-eight years old. The father of my child did not want us any longer, so he disappeared from the scene. My little girl, however, brought great satisfaction to my life. But there was always something missing.

The urgency to be in a relationship never left me. I believed that I could not handle the pressures of life on my own. I felt that I needed someone to take care of us and didn't know how I could live this life with just my daughter and me. I was in and out of relationships. Some of them were meaningful, and some were not.

In 2002, my coworkers and I went on a trip to Mexico. It was there that I met my second husband. He was from New Jersey and was also vacationing in Mexico. We kept in touch over the next year, and then decided to get married. My main reason for marrying him was for my daughter's sake. I felt she needed a father figure in her life, and he was a nice guy. I did not marry for love. We made it until 2005, when we had our son. Shortly after that, I started divorce proceedings.

It was not until years later that I understood the consequences of my behavior and their lifelong effects. I had commitment issues; I was angry; I had terrible relationships with my family members, especially with my dad; I was unfriendly toward my coworkers; I had an attitude that I was better than everyone else.

Still being single, I continued to look for happiness in futile relationships. While in these relationships, I was overwhelmed by guilt and condemnation. Because I felt so much anger toward my dad, I would consciously and unconsciously blame him for everything that had gone wrong in my life. I blamed him for my feelings of worthlessness. I went through times of feeling sorry for myself, even though I didn't realize I was doing that at the time. Questions like, "Why me? Am I unlovable? Am I not good-looking enough? Am I not worthy to be happy?" went through my mind. I saw other people living in God's blessings. I knew I wanted that, but that meant I would have to give up control. I knew I was not ready for that commitment. For years, I lived with longing and a void in my life. How could I trust that God knew what I needed?

When my daughter was a baby, I was listening to a Christian radio station one day. They were advertising an event in which you could sponsor a child who would run a marathon for Compassion Canada. The request put forth by the broadcaster was for a child by the name of Lawrence. He was eight years old, and if he didn't get a sponsor, he would be out of the program. My hard heart went out to this boy, with a sense of urgency. I signed up and sponsored him for the marathon. I did not know it at the time, but this would prove to be a life-changing experience for me. Lawrence is from Uganda, and at that moment, I became very interested in the continent of Africa.

In 2011, it was announced at the church I was attending (not my dad's church) that there was a team going to Uganda, Africa. I was asked to join the team, and with no hesitation, I accepted. There were thirty-five people on the team. We were going to build a schoolhouse and the teacher's quarters, and also, we were going to meet our sponsored children. A few significant things happened before I left for this trip. I got fired from my job. I did not foresee this coming at all. I was also in a relationship with a gentleman at the time, and he too was going to Africa, but he was going to the Congo.

We departed on June 1, 2011. Africa is one of the most beautiful places, yet the poorest place I have ever seen. The love that the people there have for the Lord is so true. If they sneezed and you said, "Bless you," they would stop and thank you for blessing them. As we made our way to the Watoto village to continue building, there were conversations taking place all around me. There was talk of poverty, the smell of Africa, the busy streets and the livestock roaming freely, and all sorts of things we would not see in Canada. As the team was observing this land, the Lord started to speak to me. He so gently showed me my daughter's life in forty years if I didn't change the way I was living. I knew exactly what He meant. I was broken. I was full of anger, loneliness, and depression and was completely empty. Well, that was it! I finally got it! At that moment, I opened the door to my heavenly Father. It was all or nothing. I had to make a decision. After this revelation, an excitement came over me to please my heavenly Father and to live righteously before my kids. I knew that He would take care of me. There was no doubt in my mind.

So many beautiful things happened in Africa. I got to see my sponsor child and family. My sponsor child's grandma told me that she prays for me every day. I never thought that having someone pray for me across the world could make such an impact on me. Her love for me changed me. I saw lots of poverty, sadness and loss, but in the midst of it all, I experienced love. I had never been so aware of God's unconditional love for me before that encounter.

When I came home, I told my boyfriend about my experience and that I chose to live righteously before my God and my children. Our relationship came to an end shortly afterward. I also did not have a job to come home to. My choice still remained to trust in God. The bills were paid, we always had food on the table, and that summer, the kids and I went to every water park in Calgary. I was out of a job for five months. Many times I went to my bank account to try and figure out how this was possible. On paper it didn't make sense. I had an assurance that He was going to take care of me. This was actually the moment He had been waiting for from me. He wanted my complete trust in Him!

I did eventually get a job in November of that year. It was a job that I didn't even apply for. This job was not my first choice, but all other opportunities did not pan out. I say that it wasn't my first choice because it was quite far from my home. Going into the interview, I had certain expectations that I needed to be met in order to make it worth my while. All of those expectations were fulfilled. With no other prospects in sight, I knew this was the job for me. The opportunities I have been afforded on this job, I would have never experienced anywhere else. We had the opportunity to host the Watoto Kid's Choir two years in a row. We were able to provide them with a full checkup, hygiene, fillings, root canals and even extraction with the specialist for these kids—free of charge.

There have been so many blessings and miracles along our journey (myself and the children). But the biggest blessing of all is the peace that I have. I have not been in a relationship with a man for two and a half years. I say that Jesus is my husband, my friend, my provider and the love of my life. I love serving Him! He has restored all of my broken relationships, but especially with my dad. I can say without a doubt that I love my dad. That was something that I could not do for the longest time. Even writing this puts a smile on my face. My change came the moment I decided to be obedient to my heavenly Father. I am not missing out on anything. My kids and I are living the abundant life. I am no longer needy...*I am loved!*

—Anonymous

The Hope of a Believing Spouse

"...As for me and my house, we will serve the Lord."
—Joshua 24:15

I WAS BORN IN WEST ALIQUIPPA, PENNSYLVANIA IN 1953, the son of Nicola and Laura (Cercone) Giuliani. My Italian immigrant father died in his sleep when I was two years of age. My mother lived until 1979, but the family always struggled under financial hardship and the spiritual oppression of poverty. My father suffered from alcoholism, which caused my mother to tell many dark stories illustrating the grip that disease had on the family. I was always encouraged as a young child that hard work would allow me to someday attend college and avoid having to work in the difficult conditions of the steel mill that provided a living to my father and older brother, Nick.

In 1975 that encouragement came to fruition when I became the first in my family to graduate from college. On the day I graduated, I also started as an accountant in the budget department of a medium-sized coal company in Indiana, Pennsylvania. A few years later, after attending graduate school at night while working full time for the coal company, I earned an MBA degree in finance.

During college, I met Nancy Davis, who became my wife in 1978. It was Nancy who introduced me to the idea of a personal relationship with my Lord and Savior, Jesus Christ. I had grown up Roman Catholic, and although I sensed the presence of the Holy Spirit during church services as a child, I had never really accepted Jesus into my heart. Nancy was always encouraging me to "give my struggles over to Jesus," a phrase I did not quite understand at the time. For many years, I had resisted a dependence on Christ because I was always taught to "work hard, keep your nose clean, and good things will happen for you." The gospel of grace was difficult for me to accept because it renders self-pride obsolete.

Nancy and I had three boys and a girl during the 1980s and early 1990s. Nancy saw my struggle as I tried to be a father while establishing myself in a business career for which I was ill-prepared from a socioeconomic standpoint. Outside of Nancy's father, I had no family members to reach out to for business advice. Early in our marriage, Nancy had committed herself to Jesus, and had been working hard to convince me to do the same. She would read scriptures to me in the morning as I shaved before leaving for the office.

Nancy had been attending Bible studies where the presence of the Holy Spirit moved and spoke. At the time, I liked to work hard and party hard, and I wasn't exactly thrilled that my bride had become a "Jesus freak." I wanted to remain Catholic as a family, but the truth was I feared that becoming a committed Christian would mean no more fun. Nancy was looking for a charismatic church where she could experience the wisdom and power of the Holy Spirit. I threatened to leave if Nancy would not relent and follow my lead.

One day, a woman in Nancy's Bible study spoke a word from God that Nancy was nagging her husband by reading him scriptures while he shaved, and that God wanted Nancy to "get out of His way" so He could deal with me. Nancy trusted God and obeyed, and God used a series of professional circumstances to draw me closer to Him. God knew He could reach me by becoming involved in my work life, because work was the most important thing to me at the time.

Perhaps the most defining moment came when I was alone driving to Pittsburgh, Pennsylvania to attend a Pirates game with some fraternity brothers. As I drove, I was thinking about a particularly frustrating professional situation, and I realized I had met my match and could not solve the problem. In my frustration, I wept and began punching the ceiling of my car and screamed to God: "OK, I give up! I give this over to You—now fix it!"

That day I happened to be running ahead of schedule for meeting my friends, so I parked the car and sat at a bench overlooking one of Pittsburgh's three rivers. God proceeded to pour into my mind a practical seven-step plan to solve my problem. I sensed an anointing and dutifully wrote down the plan, knowing in my spirit that God had heard me and was answering the cry of my heart. Within seventy-two hours, the plan was executed and the problem was solved. I was amazed at how well the plan was accepted by even my professional opponents. I decided that if God was willing and able to solve my professional problems, there was no reason not to trust Him with everything. I then decided to fully accept Jesus into my heart and to allow Him full reign over my professional life, my family life and my spiritual life.

Today, I look back at those days and joke that the miracle was that God told Nancy to stop forcing the life of Christ on me. I reasoned, if God could stop my wife from nagging, He was certainly worthy to be believed and worshipped. The reality is that God meets us where we are, and will use our difficult circumstances, our families, our illnesses, our mistakes and even our sins like pride and self-righteousness to draw us near to Him, so that we might experience the eternal love He has for us.

Like all Christians, I have faced many challenges to my faith, but God has always been faithful to show up strong, make a way and prove His love. One day in church, the Holy Spirit moved and had me forgive my father posthumously, which led me to understand the love that Father God has for me and for my earthly father. The Holy Spirit emphasized that I had been living in bondage and fear due to an "orphan mentality," and that He has wanted me to accept Him as Father.

For as many as are led by the Spirit of God, they are the sons of God. For ye have not received the spirit of bondage again to fear; but ye have received the Spirit of adoption, whereby we cry, Abba, Father. The Spirit itself beareth witness with our spirit, that we are the children of God: and if children, then heirs; heirs of God, and joint-heirs with Christ; if so be that we suffer with him, that we may be also glorified together (Romans 8:14-17 KJV).

It has taken me a while to understand that we can live free of fear, but the following Scripture passage makes it pretty clear:

Whoever confesses that Jesus is the Son of God, God abides in him, and he in God. And we have come to know and have believed the love which God has for us. God is love, and the one who abides in love abides in God, and God abides in him. By this, love is perfected with us, that we may have confidence in the day of judgment; because as He is, so also are we in this world. There is no fear in love; but perfect love casts out fear, because fear involves punishment, and the one who fears is not perfected in love. We love, because He first loved us (I John 4:15-19 NASB).

According to Strong's Concordance, the word *perfected* means to "complete... accomplish...or consummate."

If we have fear, we are not fully possessing the love that Jesus has for us.

Turning our hearts toward Jesus' love is the key to our spiritual walk.

Over the years, I have learned that being a Christian does not mean living a perfect life, but instead it means knowing that God is quick to forgive our sins when we repent and turn our hearts toward the mercy and love of His only begotten Son, Jesus. I am not perfect, and I am no more deserving of God's favor than anyone else. We don't earn His favor; instead, it is a free gift.

God has taught me to walk in integrity and peace even in the most difficult of professional circumstances. There is a peace that He has for all of us, but it begins in our heart, in our love relationship with Jesus. I encourage you today to accept Jesus Christ in your heart first, and yield to Him as He heals and changes your heart. You will experience many awesome changes, as I did. If you have already accepted Christ as Lord and Savior, I encourage you to recommit your heart to Him, and trust Him to bring back the peace you are longing for.

—Bill Giuliani

Hope for Dreams Fulfilled

*"When the Lord turned again the captivity of Zion, we were
like them that dream. Then our mouth was filled with laughter,
and our tongue with singing: then said they among the heathen,
The Lord hath done great things for them."*
—Psalms 126:1-2 (KJV)

RECEIVED CHRIST AS MY SAVIOR BACK IN 2006, TWO DAYS
after I left my abusive husband. At the time, I didn't know I was
praying a prayer of salvation. I was instead completely overwhelmed with all the responsibilities that had fallen onto my
shoulders in an instant—from getting my life in order, to taking
care of my son, who was a one and a half at the time. I was desperately seeking an answer because after my ex was no longer in
the picture, I had to face reality. I realized I had given my power
away to him for years, and I was not even close to the dreams I
had for myself at thirty years of age.

I went to the library and borrowed many self-help books.
I read about twenty-three books in one month, but was left
more confused than ever. So I decided to lay all the books on
my bedroom floor and get rid of those that didn't mention
God. I was left with just a couple of books. I put them away and
decided to open the Bible I kept all this time on my bedside
table. I have had this Bible all my life, but I had never read it.
I saw it more as a good-luck charm. That day I opened it, and
I read a scripture about excessive drinking. I had no problems
with alcohol, but I knew someone who did, and I said to myself, "If this person reads this, he may be able to kick the habit
for good." Then something happened within me. At that moment I realized the Bible was not a book about old stories with
people who served God, but a manual for living. I had finally
found the book from which all truth derives!

That same night, I decided to give my life to Christ. I was too
tired and too emotionally, mentally, financially and physically

drained to do something for myself, but I knew God would do something for me. I knew He had a plan for me, and I accepted whatever He had in store. It has been a seven-year journey through the desert, as it has been one of the hardest seasons of my life. But it has also been a season full of miracles and God's provision.

I decided to forgive my ex right away, as well as forgive myself for all of the mistakes of my past. I went back to school and finished my bachelor's degree and obtained a master's in Human Services. I quit smoking and learned how to become more organized. At the time, I was living in New Jersey, but God closed that door and brought me back to the place of my birth and my family, Puerto Rico. But best of all, God led me to get in touch with what my heart was really saying.

Ever since I was a child, I had a dream of becoming an actress. Here I was, a thirty-three-year-old single mother dreaming about being in movies! I desperately asked God to remove those dreams because I felt they were just impossible to accomplish. But the dream kept growing until I accepted the fact that God does call you to do things you enjoy. So I went back to school, and last December I completed an MFA in creative writing, with a specialization in screenwriting. At this moment, I have two scripts for short films written, a feature film script, and a play. I lead the film and theater ministry in my church, and we are getting ready to shoot our first short film and produce the play at the end of the year.

I had to learn to trust God for provision all these years. He has never been late! I know that for me a new season is starting now, and I'm finally on the verge of living the life God intended for me to have."

For those single moms who are struggling and can't see a way out, all I can say is, "Just keep going! Embrace every dream and keep going!"

—*VicMarie Del Valle*

Hope in the Healer

"And Jesus went forth, and saw a great multitude, and was moved with compassion toward them, and he healed their sick."
—Matthew 14:14 (KJV)

MANY YEARS AGO, I HAD A SIMPLE SPUR REMOVED IN my foot by an orthopedic surgeon. It left my leg swollen up to twice its size, and I could not walk. I was diagnosed with RSD (reflex sympathetic dystrophy). It was a nerve condition, which leaves the sufferer in chronic pain. People with this disease usually end up in wheelchairs. I was constantly crying in pain, and one day my daughter asked me if I had checked with God about receiving a healing.

I had not done this because my upbringing taught me that if something was wrong in my life, I deserved it and needed to find out what was inside of me that needed correcting. I followed her advice and cried out to the Lord for help. That prayer was a turning point in my life.

It took nine months before I returned to work. My healing was a process. Even though I did not know the Bible, I knew Jesus was at work in me. I pressed myself to the limit in walking. At times I took extreme measures just so I would not experience pain. One time I filled up the washing machine with ice and soaked my foot in it. Other times I would soak my foot in hot water, and then later in ice water just so I could get some relief in my body. I would pray as I would walk fast, even though that caused pain. I pressed on. I returned to work and made studying the Bible a priority in my life.

Years later, I was on a pill called Effexor. The physician used it for pain. I was growing stronger in His Word and was contending for my complete healing. One day while still in pain, I was ascending the stairs and cried out once again for Jesus to heal my body. That is when it happened! In that instant I was completely healed! Sometimes healing comes in an instant; while other times it is a process of pressing on with anticipation until healing arrives. A prayer delayed is not a prayer denied!

—Fran Carter

Hope for the Opening of Our Ears

*"And looking up to heaven with a deep sigh, He said to him,
'Ephphatha!' that is, 'Be opened!' And his ears were opened..."*
—*Mark 7:34-35*

DURING THE BEGINNING OF 2009, I BECAME VERY AWARE that I could not hear very well. I had sensed for a long time that I had partial hearing loss, and it kept getting worse. I could not hear the TV or radio very well, and quite often had to ask people to repeat what they had spoken.

I went to my family doctor. He informed me I had pressure on my eardrums and proceeded to treat me for a three-month timeframe for what he thought to be an ear infection. Three different in-office tests confirmed the fact that I indeed had pressure on my eardrums. He also tested my hearing for any loss, and confirmed on two separate occasions that I had 50 percent hearing loss. My body did not respond to the two 30-day rounds of antibiotics. There was no improvement on the pressure on my eardrums or in my loss of hearing. He then referred me to an ear, nose and throat specialist (ENT).

The ENT examined my past medical history and records, had a long consultation with me and then told me I had permanent damage to my eustachian tubes. This damage was due to the thirty-nine high intensity radiation treatments I had undergone for my throat cancer. He said the radiation treatments ionized some of the tissue in the eustachian tubes and that the normal flow between the ear canal and my throat was hindered by the tissue damage to the inside of the tubes.

Radiation is measured in *rads*. A 100-rad whole-body dose will kill you. When receiving cancer treatments, they collimate the area of your body exposed to the radiation. I received 8,000 rads to the specific area where the tumor was located in my throat, which included the area where my eustachian tubes are located. The radiation also burnt out my tonsils. They have never grown back and almost destroyed my salivary glands. Contrary to the doctor's prognosis, I now have near normal salivary gland function.

The ENT reported the radiation treatments were causing the normal drainage from ears to throat to be blocked due to the damaged and swollen linings inside the eustachian tubes. I asked him what the treatment was for my condition. He said there was no cure for the radiation damage. It was a permanent condition.

Two days later, on Friday, October 16, I went to Dr. Gold-fedder's School of Miracles in Aiken, South Carolina. I went there to learn how we ought to pray for each other so that God can move in healing. I was sitting in the back row during class, taking notes and listening to Dr. Phil teach on healing. He was including Bible verses in his teachings.

At 6:45 P.M. as Bible verses, including Psalms 107:20 (where the Bible tells us that God has sent His Word to heal us) were being read, a very strange thing happened. I heard a loud popping sound. Both of my ears popped and I experienced a strange sensation in my body. The best way I can describe it was I heard a sound originating inside my neck. This sensation was unlike anything I have ever encountered before. It was so unusual that I wrote down the time it took place.

I didn't fully comprehend it at that moment, but I later found out that God provided me with instant and complete miraculous healing of my hearing loss! Never before had God revealed Himself in such a dramatic and awesome way to me. I never doubted that God still did miracles, but I had never had a personal one and had not gone there that night expecting one. I went there to learn how to pray for other people who are sick.

The following Thursday, I went to an audiologist in Augusta. He tested my ears in three different was: perception of tones, repeating back what I heard him say, and pressure tests on my eardrums.

He examined the results, came into the room and showed me the test results that revealed I now have perfect hearing with no loss at any frequency, that I repeated back exactly what he had spoken, and that there was no pressure on my eardrums. The audiologist, who is about the same age as I am, told me he wished that his hearing was as good as mine is. I said, "Praise God!"

In a subsequent visit with my family physician, I told him my God story. He acknowledged miracles do occur and mentioned that the AMA has documented and is studying what they label as "spontaneous healings."

God is no respecter of persons (see Acts 10:34). If He were, I know for sure that I did not earn the right to be healed. I share this with you because I really do believe all things are possible with God (see Matthew 19:26), and our faith has the power to save us (see James 5:15). I appreciate doctors, and we do occasionally need their assistance. However, I have learned and am now convinced that there are no "incurable diseases."

—*Keith Graham*

Hope for the Demonstration of His Kingdom

"And he sent them to preach the kingdom of God, and to heal the sick." —Luke 9:2 (KJV)

ABOUT THIRTY YEARS AGO, I WORKED WITH LEGISLA-TORS and others in government to put programs online and acquire funding for people with special needs. One day, I was preparing to go to speak to a man in a very influential position before heading to the state capitol. Before I left home, I felt that God wanted to do something very special through me that day, and I let Him know that I was available to be used however He desired to do so.

I got to Walt's office, and he seemed to sense I was there for something very important. He arranged it so that we would not be interrupted. I was aware that Walt had a rare blood disease, but I had no idea how advanced it was. I felt impressed to tell him that he and his wife needed to begin to have daily devotionals each morning and that God was going to heal him of his blood disease. A great peace filled the room, and I felt that was God confirming His Word.

The next day, Walt and a colleague of his were standing by the window in his office, and Walt was telling him about what had transpired the day before and that he knew he was healed. It was not raining, but God put a beautiful rainbow across the sky as a confirmation.

Walt returned to the doctor who had told him he had less than two months to live, but instead confirmed that he was now totally healed! Twenty-five years went by. Walt continued to do God's work for those with special needs. He later retired. During those years, he displayed rainbows wherever he could:

in his office, home, and car, and on stationery. This was his way of thanking God. A few years after he retired, Walt went home to be with the Lord. He had finished his assignment.

—Teddye Costello

There Is Hope for Deliverance

"To You they cried out and were delivered; in You they trusted and were not disappointed." —Psalms 22:5

As a result of adultery and the disintegration, thereof, of my nuclear family, I fell into a state of despair, shame and guilt that consumed me for the greater part of the years 2005 through 2009. My pain and despair were numbed only by the false illusion of a new relationship that only sank me further into self-indulgence. However, the illusion was so distorted that I felt entitled to the picture it had craftily painted.

Internally troubled and tormented, I one day pleaded with God and pressed Him to relieve me of it all and to open my eyes and heart to His path and vision for my life. On my knees, I asked for forgiveness and for a true revival of the man I was created to be. The encounter I had with God was real, yet unexplainable. Since then, it has been an everyday deliverance as He has led me into incredible insights of who I am in Him.

Today, I can rejoice in that He has restored not only my relationship with my two sons, but also a great functional relationship with my ex-wife and mother of our sons. I finally learned how to forgive myself, which proved to be a difficult thing for me to do. My greatest joy is found in my relationship with Him that goes beyond any explanation. And that relationship is only possible because of His love, His mercy and His sacrifice. Through it all, He protected all those He placed in my care as He weaved His grace over my life. I am forever grateful and thankful.

—Doc

Hope Continually

"But as for me, I will hope continually, and will praise You yet more and more. My mouth shall tell of Your righteousness and of Your salvation all day long; for I do not know the sum of them." —Psalms 71:14-15

IN 2003, I WAS AFFLICTED WITH A TERRIBLE, INDESCRIBABLE disease in my mouth. My mouth was filled with sores, and worst still, my tongue was decaying. There was virtually no hospital within my reach that I did not go to, but the illness defied all medical solutions. All my friends and relatives abandoned me. All seemed hopeless.

It was in this place of hopelessness that I came in contact with the Word of God, and I gave my life to Christ. Not too long after my conversion, Christ showed up and restored my health. After a time of intensive prayers, I went to bed and had a dream. In the dream a man in a white gown came into my room along with two medical doctors carrying mobile surgical equipment. The man with the white gown on asked me to lie on the bed and ordered the doctors to operate on me. He stood by and gave them instructions on how to perform the surgery on me. The operation was successful, and when I woke up from my dream, I felt so light in my mouth and knew with every fiber of my being that God had intervened on my behalf.

Today, I am completely healthy and faithfully serving the Lord as a Christian here in Nigeria. I have come to know that nothing is impossible with God! His love for us is beyond comprehension. I am eternally grateful to Him!

—*Milton O. T.*

A First-Fruit Offering Brings Hope

"For on My holy mountain, on the mountain height of Israel, says the Lord God, there all the house of Israel, all of them in the land, shall serve Me. There will I [graciously] accept them, and there will I require your offerings and the firstfruits and the choicest of your contributions, with all your sacred things."
—Ezekiel 20:40 (AMP)

IN 2007, I WAS DIAGNOSED WITH CANCER. IT WAS AT THIS time, also, that I first joined the church I am currently a member of. Pastor Steve Munsey came to our church and taught on the first-fruit offering. I had been a faithful tither and gave offerings, but I did not understand the complete meaning of the first-fruit offering and all the promises that God gave His children in that special feast.

Deep in my heart, I knew I needed to do something extraordinary, and I gave $5,000. Truly, it was not an easy thing for me to do, but I just knew it was something that I had to do. I was not trying to "buy my healing" from God, but I was concerned about my children's well-being after I was gone. My youngest son came with me that night, and he had just received his first paycheck for two weeks of work. He had not even had time to cash his check yet, but he was so touched by the preaching that he gave it all.

The following week was my surgery to remove the cancer. It was supposed to last six hours at the most, but it actually lasted over thirteen hours. The doctors could not remove all the cancer because it had already spread to the lymphatic system. During the surgery, a portion of my tongue had to be removed, so after the surgery, I could no longer speak clearly. Due to the length of the surgery, I lost a big chunk of hair from the back of my head. The specialist said that it would not grow back again because the follicles had died.

During this time, I became very intimate with the Lord and was not afraid of dying anymore. A few months after the surgery, I was diagnosed with Stage 4 cancer, which had spread to my liver and lungs. The funny thing is that I was actually excited about going home to be with the Lord and seeing Him face to face. I would often find myself daydreaming about the moment that would happen.

April 2013 will be the six-year anniversary of my surgery, and I am cancer-free! My speech has been completely restored and my hair has grown back. That is not all! The same year of my surgery, the Lord gave me a house seemingly out of nowhere. I did not have to put a single penny down for it. I was not even looking for another house! At that time, I did not realize how God was blessing me. Little did I know that the economy was about to take a downward spiral. This house is my home today, and it has been a total blessing to me, and others as well.

I made a choice to trust in God completely with all my finances and not worry about money anymore. Instead, I have a knowing that He is my provider. Now I have a peace of mind that I never had before. Believe me, this was not my nature. Only God could change me from the inside out. It is exciting to live this way; resting in God in the things that before seemed impossible. With God all things are made possible. All I can say is, my God is real, and He set me up in order to bless me!

Since that first time I gave in that special offering, I have made it a habit of giving a first-fruits offering every year and the Lord has continued to bless me. He even provides the money for me to give in the offering. My whole life is a miracle. Money just seems to show up out of nowhere—inside the house and even in my checking account! My heart's desire is to know Him even more! He is so good!

—Denisse Graciela Bustinza

Hope to Live Life Again

"Trust in the Lord with all thine heart; and lean not unto thine own understanding. In all thy ways acknowledge him, and he shall direct thy paths." —Proverbs 3:5-6 (KJV)

IN 2007, I WAS EMPLOYED AS A COMMERCIAL MOTOR coach driver. On October 6, I was in Washington, D.C., which was 400 miles from home. At 4:00 A.M., I received a phone call that my house was on fire. Four hours later, my son called and said, "Mom didn't make it out."

For a short season, my life seemed to just stop. In April of the following spring, around 4:00 A.M., I heard the Lord say in my spirit, "Let's play a game of cards. Hold up your hand. This is your hand. Can you change it?"

I said, "Tell me, Lord."

He said, "Your hand only affects others when you lay a card face up on the table. This is the hand you have been dealt. Choose to play it well." I began to immediately live life again after that encounter with Him.

—*Chet Woodward*

Hope in His Benefits

"Bless the Lord, O my soul, and all that is within me, bless His holy name. Bless the Lord, O my soul, and forget none of His benefits; who pardons all your iniquities, who heals all your diseases; who redeems your life from the pit, who crowns you with lovingkindness and compassion; who satisfies your years with good things, so that your youth is renewed like the eagle."
—Psalms 103:1-5

BACK IN 1982, I WAS DIAGNOSED WITH CANCER. I HAD A couple of operations and endured six months of chemotherapy treatments. Upon returning to the hospital for a checkup, we were informed that the cancer was still present. I had nearly been killed by the chemo, so I wasn't much interested in taking any more. The doctors wanted me to take six more months of chemo and follow that with radiation treatments.

It was at this time that my heavenly Father communicated to me that if I would stand on Psalms 103:1-5, He would heal me! I know I had read this scripture before, but never with this degree of revelation! By God's grace, I was able to stand! I left Baptist Hospital and never returned! At that time, my children were two, six and seven. Our children are now married and have children of their own! God has been so faithful!

—Linda Hyland

Hope to Become Fully New

"For we walk by faith, not by sight."
—II Corinthians 5:7 (NKJV)

WAS RAISED IN CHURCH ALL MY LIFE. I ALWAYS WANTED TO do the right thing, love God and love people, but I was bound by insecurities and fears. I thought, "If I only pray more, read the Word more, worship more, then God would be pleased with me." I remember hearing and believing to some extent that God loves me, but I would not share that with other people because I felt like a hypocrite. How could I tell someone else that God loved him, when I didn't even believe it myself?

In the summer of 1997, I was involved with a ministry that had split off from another ministry, so there were many roles to fill. I had my hand in children's church, the praise team, work parties, all the services and in anything they needed help with. I made myself available. In my own way, I was trying to offset my feelings of low self-worth, but I was trapped. I knew I was trapped, but I didn't know how to break out.

Communication breakdowns began to occur between the pastor's family and me, in a major way. This was extremely painful for me as I had made them, in my mind, the family I didn't have. I didn't know the term *codependent* at the time, but as I look back, I can see how codependent I really was. It was as if God began to remove all of my external props from under my feet, or more accurately, my heart.

At one point, the emotional pain was so great that I felt as though I couldn't take it anymore. I fell on my knees on my kitchen floor and cried out to God from a deep place: a place in me that I didn't even know existed. It was as if God broke through the corridors of the hell that surrounded me and rescued my heart. For the first time ever, I knew that God loved me; that God, the creator of the universe, loved Tonya completely and unconditionally! The emptiness left. My heart was full. My mind was at peace. The grace and love of God had touched a deep place within me, and I knew I would never be the same.

Here's the thing, I accepted Christ as my Lord and Savior when I was a senior in high school and I received the baptism of the Holy Spirit in 1987. I do not want to diminish either of those experiences; but in 1997, I felt in my spirit that this is what it is really like to be born again! The journey for me of living the Christian life from the inside out began that day, and I have never looked back!

—*Tonya Hedrick*

Hope in the One True God

"The Lord our God is one Lord: and thou shalt love the Lord thy God with all thine heart, and with all thy soul, and with all thy might." —Deuteronomy 6:4-5 (KJV)

I THANK GOD FOR HEALING ME OF A VERY AGGRESSIVE form of inflammatory breast cancer that went from Stage 1A to Stage 3B within three weeks.

I was diagnosed on December 20, 2010 after having a biopsy done. On January 20, 2011, I underwent surgery after an MRI showed that I had a total of three masses. Had it not been for the location of one tumor, I would not have known I had cancer, since the mammogram did not show the masses that were deep within the breast.

God, in His mercy, helped me through the difficulties of the chemo treatments. Each chemo treatment was so strong that I had to be put to sleep during the treatment. Within two weeks, I lost my hair. I determined in my heart that I would not offend God by asking the "whys," but instead my sister, Myriam, who was my caregiver, and I purposed in our hearts to pray for others. Every night at ten, she would read a chapter of the Book of Job and from the Psalms, and we would pray for the needs of others. Often she would do the praying because I would be too sick to even pray. I also purposed in my heart to take communion every night (the bread and juice) and read Isaiah 53.

In spite of my difficulties from the chemotherapy treatments, the doctors were amazed at my blood test results and how well I was doing in spite of how sick I was. They knew of my strong faith in God.

On Mother's Day, May 8, 2011, I was healed. After each treatment, I would go through a ten-day period of constant pain for which I had to take pain medication. The medication would make me sleep, for only a few hours during the night or day.

On this particular night, I was experiencing quite a bit of pain along with a few other physical things. Through the night, as was my custom, I kept saying, "Lord Jesus, You are my healer." Around five o'clock in the morning, my body felt a release. I slept about another hour. I always waited for my sister to get up before I would arise because I didn't want to interrupt her devotional time with the Lord. That morning when I got up, I was pain-free! Praise the Lord! When she asked me how I felt, I told her that I was pain-free because God had healed me. She asked me what I meant. I told her I was healed and I felt no pain. I was drugged by the medications, but I had no pain in my body.

I knew in my spirit I had received my healing that morning, but I had to finish the chemo treatments. I went through thirty-three treatments of radiation along with the chemo treatments. I knew I was healed and would testify to the doctors of that certainty and continued to praise the Lord.

After the radiation treatments were finished, I was put on oral preventive chemo for five years to prevent the cancer from returning to another part of my body. That medication made me ill, and finally I said I am healed and didn't take any more medication. Praise the Lord! On my last three-month check up, November 27, 2012, twenty-three months and seven days after being diagnosed with cancer, the oncologist and radiologist declared me to be cancer-free! My response to them was, "I know God healed me!" I am currently recuperating and even though it is a slow process, I thank God for not having to take any medications. He is faithful! As He has done for me, He will do for you! He is the Great Physician!

—*Elizabeth Perez*

Hope to Just Be Me

"But now there are many members, but one body....and those members of the body, which we deem less honorable, on these we bestow more abundant honor...." —I Corinthians 12:20,23

I WAS RAISED IN A CHRISTIAN HOME IN OKLAHOMA. I'M sixty-seven now. It was with awe and wonder that I married a preacher. He and I have passed through dark waters and majestic heights. When we were first married, we came from different backgrounds. He had grown up in an alcoholic home with lots of music. He started playing in bands by the age of fourteen. I had only known church and lots of it. He was saved at nineteen.

We started ministering immediately after marriage, which is now fifty years ago. He knew the Word, but I knew nothing about ministry. I tried to imitate my former pastors' wives at the start. I couldn't live up to either of them. I kept having this dream that I was sitting at the organ and all of a sudden, I became almost naked with my underwear showing. I couldn't figure out how to leave and get my clothes on. I would wake up in a panic. I had this dream for years.

Finally after many years, I took a long look at myself and decided that I was a good person, unique and loveable. *I love people!* Then I told myself that if people didn't love me for my true self, instead of those I was trying to portray, then that was too bad for them. I started trusting myself with people, decisions and friendships. The Lord helped me be *me!* I never had that dream again.

I believe it was a dream that was fear-based—that if people found out what I was really like, they wouldn't like me. This was a lie from the pit of hell! It was a dream of disclosure. I praise Jesus that He found me in my insecurity and delivered me from it! I am so not perfect by any stretch of the imagination, but I'm free from the fear of being exposed and the enemy keeping me in the lie he told me over and over. It is just like Jesus to heal every part of us so we are free to help others through the same things.

—*Vada F. Allen*

Hope for a Marriage to Be Turned Around

"For the unbelieving husband is sanctified by the wife, and the unbelieving wife is sanctified by the husband: else were your children unclean; but now are they holy."
—I Corinthians 7:14 (KJV)

RECENTLY, MY HUSBAND AND I WENT THROUGH A VERY difficult time. He became surrounded in darkness and felt that he didn't want to be married to me anymore. He could not see how our relationship could be any better or different and lacked the desire to even try to find a way. Eventually, he had an affair and then became so tormented about the people he was hurting and the mess he had made that he didn't see a way out. He then attempted to commit suicide. He was interrupted though, and did not follow through with it. Thank God! I know that it was because of my constant prayers for my husband that his life was saved. Even though I had no idea of all that he was going through or that he had planned this, God used my prayers.

Through the encouragement of a friend who had stood for her marriage for eleven years, I found Rejoice Ministries and spoke the Stander's Affirmation (posted on their website) over my marriage every day. I prayed for my husband's healing and restoration to the Father and for the restoration of our marriage.

There were days when I would lie on the floor and sob and think that I could not possibly go on. Each time, God would cover me with His peace, even in the midst of my storm. My friend gave me scriptures to pray. She and others encouraged me, prayed for me and for our marriage, listened to and wept with me. Those precious sisters held me up when I could not stand on my own.

One of them told me about a week-long ministry intensive in California called *Freedom Through Forgiveness,* and with the help of her husband, I managed to convince my husband to go. At this point, neither of us had much hope that it would help, but I clung to the possibility and continued to pray and tried to encourage my husband. Finally, after waiting nine long weeks to go, our time came. My husband later told me that he figured he would go even though he really didn't want to; and after we got back, he would file for divorce.

For the first couple of days, nothing seemed to happen. Then at the end of the third day, I began to see my husband returning to himself. The darkness began to lift, and he started to feel hopeful again. By the fourth evening, there was a marked difference. He even told me he felt lighter and that the darkness that had been a constant presence in his life had lifted. The last day we were there, we had a major breakthrough for us as a married couple and have been able to take that healing and growth and move forward into a marriage that is better now than it ever was!

Through prayer and trust in God, He was able to turn an impossible situation around and bring healing and strength. I know that without God, none of that would have been possible. He gave me strength to stand for my husband and my marriage and brought changes and healing in my husband and myself and ultimately restored our marriage! Truly, with God all things are possible to him who believes!

—Cami Lewis

Hope in the Face of Challenge

*"For You formed my inward parts; You wove me in my
mother's womb. I will give thanks to You, for I am fearfully
and wonderfully made; wonderful are Your works, and my soul
knows it very well." —Psalms 139:13-14*

YES! YOU, O LORD, SHAPED ME FIRST INSIDE AND THEN outside. You formed me in my mother's womb!

I was born a handicapped girl with physical challenges. I have not always been able to keep up with others because of that. My whole life has been based on Psalms 139:13. God has always been there to take care of me no matter what path I have had to walk. People have made fun of me and children have teased me, and it has hurt my feelings.

The hardest physical challenge I have endured was going blind in my right eye at the age of fourteen. I have not driven a car for nine years now. So the question is, do I totally have faith in the God who is the healer of my body? Yes, because He has and is touching me physically. If His creating me this way brings Him glory, then I accept that He loves me just the way I am!

—*Pam Dishon*

Hope in the Giver of Life

"For God so loved the world, that He gave His only begotten Son, that whosoever believeth in Him should not perish, but have everlasting life." —John 3:16 (KJV)

WHEN I WAS PREGNANT WITH MY SECOND CHILD BACK in 2002, I was threatening a miscarriage. I was in much pain starting at two months, and it lasted for the duration of my pregnancy. At around six months into my pregnancy, I was placed on bed rest. Even while lying down, I experienced much pain. Around that time, I was admitted into the hospital where they continuously worked to stop my labor. They did multiple ultrasounds. However, one particular ultrasound came back with devastating news. They said I was experiencing uterus abruption, which occurs when the placenta detaches from the uterus and the child looses oxygen in the blood. Most babies are stillborn when this happens, or they may suffer severe brain damage. The doctors told me they had to deliver the baby as soon as possible. They gave me all types of shots to strengthen the baby's lungs and to ensure that she would be as strong as possible before the delivery. They performed ultrasounds around the clock. They wanted to keep the baby in the womb as long as possible.

My husband and I stood in agreement, along with other family members, that God could perform a miracle. A few days had passed, which seemed unbelievable to my doctor because he informed us that once the abruption process begins, it usually is a short time before delivery. They did a final ultrasound and were astonished at their findings. The placenta had reattached to the uterine wall. That was unheard of! When my doctor came into my room, he sat down on my bed and held his head. He said it was impossible for something like this to occur. We were not shocked at all! We told him that what looks impossible with man is always possible with God! I don't know where his faith stood before, but on that day, he believed!

I was discharged from the hospital. Even though I was still having many contractions and was hospitalized to stop labor quite a few more times, I gave birth to my daughter the first day of my ninth month. She was five pounds three ounces, with very strong lungs.

This has not been the only time I have seen God do the impossible in my life. I joined the Army in 2005 and I was a very healthy and fit soldier. I took Ibuprofen here and there for shin splints from running, but that was it. I also took oral medication for acne. As it turned out, the acne medication began causing fluid to build up in my head. I was diagnosed with pseudotumor cerebri/hydrocephalus tumor in 2007. As of this date, I have had ten brain surgeries to drain the fluid. Back in 2007, I was on a lot of medication with many side effects and I began having really bad abdominal pains.

I remember going to one of my appointments and walking down the hall. With every step, it felt like something was pulling me down. I began to walk bent over so the pulling wouldn't be so bad. It got worse. I had multiple things working against me: a massive headache, crazy muscle spasms in my back and legs (probably from all the spinal taps) and sciatica. I also suffered interstitial cystitis (a bladder condition) and had numbness in my hands and feet.

After walking bent over for so long, and still in great pain, the Army issued me a wheelchair. I was in physical therapy twice a week. It didn't help. I had laparoscopy surgeries that didn't show anything. The only time I could straighten out was in the pool. I never wanted to become dependent on the wheelchair, so I forced myself to walk around the house and only use the chair for long distances outside of the home. It took a couple of years, but now I can walk freely. I still may have pains here and there when I walk, but I no longer need the chair. I am believing that He who began a good work in me shall complete it!

—*Lakeyshia Tate*

Hope for the Bound

"And this is life eternal, that they might know thee the only true God, and Jesus Christ, whom thou hast sent."
—John 17:3 (KJV)

SUPERNATURAL PHENOMENA INTERESTED ME SINCE CHILDHOOD. A few psychic episodes as a child added to the intrigue I felt. My mother had also experienced psychic events since her childhood, but didn't pursue it seriously until later. By the time I began middle school, she felt ready to experiment further. When walking her dogs in the park one day, a medium approached, telling Mom he saw her potential as a medium and invited her to a spiritualist church in Glasgow, Scotland, where we lived.

Very quickly, Mom became totally engrossed by the supernatural. As a new member of the spiritualist church, she attended Sunday services, midweek psychic development groups and Yoga classes. She shared everything she learned with me, and I also became fascinated. Her heart's desire was to train in mediumship, and other mediums encouraged this, asking her to join an open circle to learn to meditate and channel spirits of the deceased. Mom was keen to develop her abilities of clairvoyance, clairaudience and clairsentience and to learn from other mediums.

Every time Mom booked a private sitting for a life reading with a resident or visiting medium, she would buy a recording of the session, and we'd listen to it later that day. It amazed me that a half-hour recording could contain so much communication from spirits. Minute details were relayed about our lives. Precise names, places and dates were often given. It was obvious the mediums weren't charlatans, falling upon names by sheer chance. They accurately described the physical appearances, personalities and even repeated common phrases of our apparent dead relatives as they supposedly conversed with them.

I also joined the spiritualist church in Glasgow. Mom and I devoured mystical books on Yoga, opening the chakras, crystal healing, reincarnation, alternative therapies, etc. Attending New Age centers and psychic fairs, we absorbed as much information as we could to help in our spiritual enlightenment. With our passion for environmental and conservation concerns, social justice and international peace, we gladly participated in attempting to heal people and animals, through either contact or distant psychic healing.

Eventually, we attended transfiguration sessions. Mom developed in the area of automatic writing. Mediums predicted I'd become an author on behalf of spirit guides and a psychic artist, drawing portraits of dead relatives and spirit guides for clients. I experimented with Kirlian photography; using infrared film, I captured images of ectoplasm as it formed.

Over the next ten years, we'd often hear of mediums who could no longer control when spirits spoke to or through them. Many mediums had nervous breakdowns. Some attacked people claiming their spirit guides had forced them to, or were admitted to psychiatric wards. We heard reports of poltergeist activity in mediums' homes. At first, we accepted explanations that mischievous or obnoxious spirits could sometimes come through, and it was a potential hazard of the job. But when it happened to us, it became difficult to tolerate and made it almost impossible to function properly.

Our beloved friends, the other psychics and mediums, kindly tried, but failed to free our home from spirits. The spirits spoke to Mom constantly, depriving her of sleep, attacking her physically, clapping loudly from within closets, slamming all the doors, etc.

On one occasion, they forced her into a trance against her will while she was frying food. When she came out of the trance, the kitchen was consumed by fire. I arrived home after the firemen had extinguished it, just before it spread to other rooms. We all realized Mom, our dogs and cats could have been killed. One afternoon, Mom's elderly aunt who had also visited spiritualist churches, felt invisible hands grab her and throw her down our stairs. Her wrist was broken. Another day, while approaching shops, I watched in horror as Mom was lifted from the ground and catapulted from the pavement, landing on the hood of a passing car. This particular incident happened more than once.

We decided to withdraw from spiritualism and told our spirit guides to leave. To our shock, they laughed and insulted us. They began to physically attack us. This was perplexing, as they had provided guidance and kindness for many years. It became obvious they had deceived us, pretending to be benevolent, when in reality they were wicked all along.

The biggest shock, however, came when even our supposedly "dead relatives" turned against us. They also mocked and hit us. The spirits warned we couldn't leave the occult, as we had unknowingly given them control from the first day we invited them into our lives. It became clear to Mom and me that there was something not right about spiritualism, if even the mediums who had brought our "spirit friends" to us had not discerned their true identity.

Susan, a Christian I'd met in a psychology tutorial at university, invited me to her Pentecostal church, explaining that other psychics who had experienced similar tragedies were set free from spiritual attacks when they accepted the biblical Jesus Christ as their Savior (not the New Age false Christ). I renounced spiritualism and became a Christian.

During my second year at university, Mom's health deteriorated and her spirit guides threatened to use her to kill people. Mom's doctor couldn't accept poltergeist activity and diagnosed her as schizophrenic. Mom was detained in a psychiatric hospital, much to our utter shock.

Although my Mom gave her heart to Jesus a few months later, the church I had joined had no experience at that point in helping people like Mom. At that time, they didn't have the deliverance ministry. As a baby Christian myself, I didn't yet know there were Christians who could have cast those demons out of my Mom, in Jesus' name. After months of heavy sedation, the psychiatrists discharged her, but when she returned home, she endured further harassment from the spirits. The church I belonged to didn't yet have experience of casting demons out of homes or people.

Sadly, my mother committed suicide. Although it is not rare for someone to do this, over the past seventeen years I've heard of many around the world affected by the New Age or occult who have been in psychiatric wards or killed themselves. Therefore, I feel it emphasizes the crucial importance for Christians to embrace the deliverance ministry and be God's instruments to bring freedom to such tortured people, in Jesus' name. Over the years as a Christian, I have been honored and delighted that the Holy Spirit has used me to see people and homes be set free from demonic harassment. *"...Greater is He that is in you; than he that is in the world"* (I John 4:4 KJV).

Later, another pastor more experienced in deliverance prayer and casting out demons, and the co-pastor, visited my mom's home, successfully cleansing it the first time they prayed. At the name of Jesus, all the spirits left and never returned. Later, I sold Mom's home without worrying that the new tenants would be harassed.

The Pentecostal church did not portray dead religious traditions; instead it was lively, loving and fun. The members are trained by the Holy Spirit to prophesy about the future; bodies are healed and other miracles, signs and wonders occur. Actually, in a couple of years, I saw more people healed in Pentecostal churches than I ever saw in over ten years at spiritualist churches.

When I became a Christian, even before I had read the biblical warnings of the occult in Deuteronomy chapter 18, I instinctively realized what had happened. The missing piece of the jigsaw fit into place. When our "dead relatives and the spirit guides" began to attack Mom and me, it indicated they were actually evil spirits who had deceived us, merely impersonating our loved ones. It made complete sense when Christians explained that it is impossible for dead souls to return to talk with us, as they remain in heaven or hell for eternity.

Also, spirits are evil fallen angels. They've existed for centuries possessing psychic knowledge of our families and historical figures down the generations. They can easily disguise their evil form to pose as our deceased family to mimic spirit guides or any famous celebrity that ever lived. The Bible says that the entities, who work through witches, mediums, etc., are called familiar spirits, as they are psychic and very familiar with how all your ancestors looked and spoke. Thus, these entities can impersonate them perfectly. The Hebrew word for familiar spirits actually means "demon," evil spirit.

Jesus healed me of fears, phobias and physical conditions. He has given me joy and peace I simply never knew existed. His very tangible presence of pure love is more real than any powerful encounter I experienced within spiritualism.

—Laura Maxwell

As Long as There Is Breath, There Is Hope

"Why are you in despair, O my soul? And why have you become disturbed within me? Hope in God, for I shall again praise Him for the help of His presence." —Psalms 42:5

MY STORY BEGAN AT TWELVE YEARS OLD WHEN I PICKED up my first marijuana joint and smoked it with my older brother. It ended with the pregnancy of my now twenty-five year old daughter, Janar.

The "dash" in between included snorting cocaine at age seventeen, losing my mind and having to be hospitalized in mental institutions on four occasions between the ages of nineteen and twenty, losing a baby who was stillborn at six months, losing the love of my life and finally finding the Lord Jesus Christ!

My life motto has become, "As long as there is breath in your body, there is hope!" Today, I am twenty-six years in recovery and God has used me to help thousands of families overcome the devastation of addiction.

—*Rosalind Y. Tompkins*

Hope for Answered Prayer

"Truly I say to you, whoever says to this mountain, 'Be taken up and cast into the sea' and does not doubt in his heart, but believes that what he says is going to happen, it will be granted him. Therefore, I say to you, all things for which you pray and ask, believe that you have received them, and they will be granted you. Whenever you stand praying, forgive, if you have anything against anyone, so that your Father who is in heaven will also forgive you your transgressions." —Mark 11:23-25

IN 1988, MY MOTHER WAS DIAGNOSED WITH SARCOIDOSIS. Because of this disease, her spleen needed to be surgically removed. All the complications from this disease and surgery caused her to have heart and lung problems as well. So, for the following eight years, my mother was in and out of the hospital, on many medications and had to breathe using an oxygen tank. Throughout all those years, I never heard her complain about her sickness, never question God; but instead she always had a smile on her face. Her faith in God was strong, and she always said that God was going to heal her. Her life is a testament.

Fast forward to August 30, 1996. My mother decided to go on a twenty-one-day fast for her healing. She didn't take her medication or use her oxygen tank for the whole twenty-one days. She along with a few of her prayer partners prayed during the whole fast. To me, the fact that she survived twenty-one days without taking medication was a miracle in and of itself. Not only was she praying for her healing, but she was also praying for her children, grandchildren and other family members.

On September 20, 1996, she had a talk with me about a lot of things and later started singing this song, "I Know I've Been Changed." After she finished singing, she kept repeating that the angels in heaven just signed her name. She said she felt no pain. Later that night, she began vomiting black fluid and water, and I didn't know why.

The next morning, September 21, 1996, my mom passed away on the couch in the family room. When I saw her lying there, her eyes were closed and she had the biggest smile on her face I had ever seen in my life. I honestly believe she saw the face of God.

Rumors began to go around that she died from the fast, or from not taking her medication, or that maybe she had a heart attack. When we got the autopsy back, they found nothing wrong with her! Her heart and lungs were fine, and they also found a small spleen that grew back! To this day, I do not know what caused her death, but I do know that God completely healed her body!

We found out later that exactly three months before she passed, she wrote out her funeral arrangements. In her arrangements, two things stood out to me the most. One was the scripture Mark 11:23-26 and the other was something she said, and I quote: "Dance and praise the Lord for I am not dead. I am just beginning to live. I pray that you all will make it to heaven because after you meet Jesus, I will be next in line, and we will sweep through the city."

A week later, we had her funeral, which was more like a celebration. The testimony of her life was so profound that seven people gave their lives to Christ at the funeral! I can truly say that my mother was a witness and a living testimony for Christ, and He used her for His glory. Although my mother has been gone for over sixteen years now, I am still seeing God answering her prayers in my life, as well as the lives of my family.

God is such a good God. He is a healer and will answer your prayers! God will answer your prayers in His perfect timing and will use your life as a living testimony for His great purpose and glory!

—Barry Dodd

Hope When We Ask in Accordance with His Will

"Now this is the confidence that we have in Him, that if we ask anything according to His will, He hears us. And if we know that He hears us, whatever we ask, we know that we have the petitions that we have asked of Him." —I John 5:14-15 (NKJV)

DURING THE SPRING OF 2011, SEEMINGLY OUT OF THE BLUE, I was faced with two life-threatening illnesses. For eight long months, I was fighting for my life. My prostate completely closed on me and within weeks, a hard tumor the size of a football appeared in my stomach. After doctors' examinations, I was told from all the signs that it was cancer. With the reality of cancer staring me in the eyes, I refused any medical attention except for antibiotics given me for the horrible infection I suffered due to the prostate closing up. I returned home to walk out my miracle.

From the very outset of this entire event, I knew without a doubt I was going to receive a full-blown miracle in my body, even though I lived through months of great pain and horrible side effects from these diseases. It would take a book to tell the entire story of what I lived through and how I walked out my miracle. By January 2012, the tumor completely disappeared and my prostate issue cleared up. I am alive today to testify that God is a God of the miraculous. I had determined from the very beginning when these two things hit me that no knife was going to touch my body, and I would receive no chemotherapy or radiation. I was going to get a full-blown miracle instead!

I dug in my heels and refused to allow the word *cancer* to negatively affect me, or fear to enter the picture. I put my total focus on the four gospels and the ministry of Jesus Christ to the sick and diseased. Many times I would tell the Lord that

He knew if I were alive during the days He walked the earth, I would have been there on the side of that hill where they brought to Him every kind of sickness and disease, and He healed them all. I would have reached out and grabbed Him and not let Him go until He touched me. But that was 2,000 years ago and doing that today is impossible. I reminded Him that He went to a whipping post and was beaten for me so that 2,000 years later, I could be healed and am going to be healed. Every day I would say, "With my very next step, I am going to reach out and touch Jesus, and He is going to reach out and touch me."

Another prayer I prayed was, "Father, Your Son, Jesus is sitting at Your right hand. Right now look at Your Son's back. I am reminding You of all that He went through so I could be healed. Every ounce of flesh that was ripped off His body, every drop of blood that was shed, was for me. Because of what He went through, I can be healed today!" At night when I lay down, I would say to myself, "Tomorrow morning I am going to wake up healed." When I woke up the next morning not healed, I would say, "Today, I am going to reach out and touch Jesus and He is going to reach out and touch me." I knew that any second a miracle was going to take place.

As days and months went by, I refused to believe that I would not be healed. I did not go through the house quoting one scripture after another, for I did not need to convince my mind He was going to heal me. Deep within, I knew it! The scripture I stood on was First John 5:14-15: *"Now this is the confidence that we have in Him, that if we ask anything according to His will, He hears us. And if we know that He hears us, whatever we ask, we know that we have the petitions that we have asked of Him"* (NKJV).

During this whole time, I wanted and prayed for an instant miracle to take place because I wanted the pain I was living with gone from my body. But after a while when I realized this might take some time, I made up my mind that I was in this thing for the long haul. I was going to get a miracle no matter how long it was going to take. After eight months of putting my trust and confidence in God's ability to heal me, a miracle took place. I can't tell you the date my miracle took place. The only way I can explain what happened is to say that the tumor slowly shrank until it completely disappeared, and today my prostate is functioning perfectly. Jesus Christ is the same yesterday, today and forever!

—*Roger Webb*

Hope for His Reward

"Lo, children are an heritage of the Lord: and the fruit of the womb is his reward." —Psalms 127:3 (KJV)

I HAD A BEAUTIFUL DAUGHTER, BUT WANTED A SIBLING FOR HER so she would not grow up alone. I prayed and cried every month for about fourteen years. I went to more than one fertility doctor. I was finally sent to one who offered a different approach, and was told that it was possible at thirty-seven to get pregnant with the proper approach.

My friends and family members kept telling me to give up and accept the fact that God was telling me "No" in regards to my prayers for another child. But my heart was still broken; so I went to the Lord with their point of view. I heard by His Spirit deep in my heart, "Who are you going to listen to—Me or them? Trust Me!" I chose to trust the Lord, and soon after, I had a vision of a two-year old blonde boy playing outside with a little girl further back in the vision.

By July, I was pregnant with twins. It was a little girl and a little boy, but the little girl's egg did not develop properly. My beautiful miracle son was born one week before my fortieth birthday. My pregnancy and delivery were much easier than with my daughter at the age of twenty-four! God is a miracle worker!

—Pam Kemnitz

Hope for the Sick

"Is any sick among you? let him call for the elders of the church; and let them pray over him, anointing him with oil in the name of the Lord: and the prayer of faith shall save the sick, and the Lord shall raise him up..." —James 5:14-15 (KJV)

UPON MY DELIVERY FIFTY-FIVE YEARS AGO, A TEAM OF DOCTORS told my mother that I would never walk, even if I lived.

I was too young to remember my healing, but my mother told me this story many times. When I got older, I would ask her to tell me my story over and over again. She would tell me this story with such passion and detail every time that it was like I was hearing it for the first time. Little did I realize at the time of my youth that hearing this account was building my faith in God's miracle-working power and taught me to never lose hope, no matter what I faced in life.

I was born with a severe liver disease, and when I was around six months old, they performed exploratory surgery. I still have the scar today. They saw that my entire liver was covered with tiny black spots, and I had yellow jaundice as well. The doctors told my mother there was nothing they could do; my entire liver was diseased and they could not fix it.

My mother called our pastor, Zera Hampton, and she came and prayed for me. When she finished praying, she told my mother, "He is going to be just fine." By the next morning, the yellow jaundice was gone and my color returned to normal. They did some more tests on my liver and found that it had begun to function normally as well. The team of doctors couldn't explain what happened.

They also had diagnosed me with rickets. This is a childhood bone disorder where the bones soften and become prone to fractures and deformity. Rickets is sometimes caused by liver problems. If I lived with the liver issue, I would never walk and the bad liver within me had already done the damage.

I was released from the hospital about a week later and was followed up with biweekly checkups, which later became monthly checkups. As the time approached for me to walk, I did! In one of our visits to the doctor, my mother told the doctor I was walking. He checked the file and said, "I'm sorry, Mrs. Warren, but your son will probably never walk. Even if he takes a few steps, his legs are not strong enough to hold his weight." My mother went on to tell the doctor that I was not just walking, but I was also running. He picked me up and took me to the other side of the room. I ran to my mother as soon as my feet hit the floor. The team of doctors was amazed and said once again that they could not explain it.

I turned fifty-five on April 13, 2013, and I have been running ever since my miracle! God healed me of both the liver disease and a bone disorder called rickets! Praise be to our God!

—Glen Warren

Hope to See Ourselves as God Sees Us

"How precious also are Your thoughts to me, O God! How vast is the sum of them!" —Psalms 139:17

My Reflection Through the Eyes of God

My reflection through the eyes of God
Allows me to see me as I really am
Not just the person on the surface,
But the one who is in the image of the Great I Am
Who has shaped and molded every part and every tone
No need for alteration or an appointment with silicone
My reflection through the eyes of God
Eyes can only see with light
Light that takes in the object giving sight
My vision often tainted
Showing me images of self that at times can seem false
To a world that makes it shameful at times
Cover my face with makeup and gloss
My reflection through the eyes of God
He sees no problem with what He has made
The lips, the thighs, the hips, the eyes
He is pleased
His creation, beautiful
His creation, wonderful
His creation, magnified
His creation, glorified
My reflection through the eyes of God
Learn to see you as He does
No concerns of what it could have been or what it was

In the now, embracing every inch of me
The eyes now seeing, what He sees

—Belinda Gammage[1]

I wrote this poem because it brought me back to a time when I struggled with so many self-esteem issues—issues that went back to when I was a little girl. Growing up, I didn't realize there was something "wrong" with my looks until I was told my nose was too big. I remember hearing this from someone close to me. What they thought was innocent—as they began to explain how I could get a nose job when I got older and then proceeded to squeeze my nose—turned into a lifetime of my feeling extremely self-conscious about my face and wishing I were different.

From there we go to the hair. I was a little black girl with pigtails. Because my natural hair was not straight and easy to manage, I had to endure the hot pressing comb. That was not a problem until the people who were doing my hair talked about how nappy it was. I wondered, "What does that mean?"

Growing up, I played with Barbie dolls. Barbie appeared to be the epitome of what was considered beautiful. Not only that, but as an eight-year-old (though I was embraced with love and care), the television also showed a different picture of what beauty was than what I saw in the mirror. Everyone on television was white. I didn't see anyone I could identify with. I don't remember a black woman that I would watch on TV and actually embrace as a role model for me. Something in me felt that being who I was simply was not good enough.

I can't pinpoint where it began, but I can say that I had an encounter with my Auntie Gloria, and my perspective began to change. Now Auntie Gloria was beautiful to me. I remember so well her dark cocoa complexion and flawless skin. She was an intelligent woman, a sharp dresser who exuded a lot of confidence. She always wore a bright, beautiful smile. One day, for some reason, I released these words: "I wish I was white."

At that time, I had to be anywhere from eight to ten years old. What made me say that? Somewhere along the way, I didn't like who God created me to be. Somewhere, I can't remember exactly where, something was said that made me feel my looks were not good enough. My aunt sat me down and reminded me of my beauty and the fact that we all come in different shades and sizes. She told me never to say that again—and I didn't, for fear of what she would say to me next!

Now we come to the present day. As an adult, I struggled with this until recently. Even at twenty-eight years old, I had developed these mental models regarding my reflection in the mirror. I looked and saw nothing beautiful about me. Low self-esteem trailed me. I remember letting a young man know how I felt about him, and he was nice about it, but he told me I was not his type. I was so hurt and made a statement in an email to a friend of mine at the time. These were my exact words: "I know I am a plus-size woman, and I know my nose is wide, so I can understand that I am not his type." Wow! I still can't believe I said this. She kindly called me on this and said that those were not the reasons at all. I really needed an internal spiritual cleansing. I had carried this false mindset that was keeping me from truly embracing the skin I was in.

After my friend coached me, I had to go through a process of seeing myself as God sees me. The way He began was amazing. He started by crowning me with jewels. The first time it happened, I was at church and a young woman said to me, "I have something for you." We went into the restroom, and she gave me two boxes of jewelry. I was floored. No one had ever done this for me before. For a long time, I would not wear a lot of jewelry; somehow I felt I just didn't deserve those things and I never purchased them. As time went on, God began to use people all around me to compliment me on how beautiful I was. My self-esteem began to rise, and as I began to see myself the way God sees me, more people began to say how beautiful I was. What was going on inside of me began to be reflected on the outside.

One day, I was in the mirror putting on makeup. The first layer for most women is the foundation. As I applied my foundation, I asked God, "What are You doing in my life? Why am I going through all of these things?"

He simply answered by saying, "I am laying a foundation." What a timely statement! He has built layer upon layer in my life. I thank God for the healing process He has taken me through. It has not been easy, but I know that I am on my way to doing great things as I embrace the beautiful woman I am inside and out. And most amazing to me is that *Belinda* means "beautiful" in Spanish. I am finally embracing my name.

—Belinda Gammage

1. Belinda Gammage, 2012 HighVolumes Multimedia LLC (HV Publishing).

Hope in the Life-Giver

"I will not die, but live, and declare the works of the Lord. The Lord hath chastened me sore: but he hath not given me over unto death." —Psalms 118:17-18 (KJV)

DURING MY PREGNANCY WITH MY THIRD SON, THERE WERE a few medical problems that caused me to be mostly bedridden for about four months during the second and third trimesters. It seemed that things were getting better, and the baby was developing properly.

During the ninth week before he was due, the doctor noticed that the baby was not turning into the proper position for delivery. Indeed, my appointment with the doctor the following week confirmed that the baby was still not in the act of turning head-down in order to be positioned properly for delivery. The doctor was concerned that we might be facing a breach birth. At the end of that week, I began having very strong contractions and was admitted into the hospital where the doctors confirmed that indeed I was in labor and the baby was soon to arrive. I was sent to the delivery room where there were better monitors than the room I was first admitted to. I called a dear pastor friend at her home very late at night and asked her to pray.

The labor intensified and I was past the point in delivery where the doctor could safely administer drugs to stop the labor. The doctor was hopeful that the contractions would stop on their own and eventually stop altogether so that the baby could continue to develop inside the womb. They continued to monitor me over the next several hours and noted that the baby still had not turned into the proper position for delivery, even though things were progressing into full delivery mode.

The baby began to show signs of distress as his heart rate was slowing down. At times it was even difficult to locate any heart rate at all. The doctor decided to administer a drug to speed up the delivery hoping to avoid the need for a Cesarean. He felt certain, also, that he would be able to turn the child during delivery to correct the breach position. However my body reacted negatively to the drug they administered and I began to experience such intense labor that the monitor began to read my contractions as off the chart. During the last hour of the delivery, the labor was so intense that the bag of water fully intact and seemingly like a water balloon, shot across the room and splattered against the wall. I heard the doctor say, "Dry birth!" The doctor was unable to turn the baby as he was now rapidly descending and I was in the last stages of delivery.

As the baby's head began to appear, the mood in the room changed from joy and relief to a building desperation. The doctor began to call for more medications to be administered to me intravenously and told the nurses to be ready to get an I.V. for the baby. Then suddenly my son was born, but he was quickly placed in a towel after the umbilical cord was cut and scurried to another part of the room out of our view. The doctor stepped over there and I waited to hear the sound of a baby crying, but heard nothing. The baby was quickly removed from the room and I heard over the loud speaker, "Code Red." I could hear footsteps in the hallway outside of my room. My husband went to the doorway, and I knew by the way he stood that something was not right. Then within a few seconds, I heard announced over the intercom a Code Blue. Nurses and medical personnel ran past the room. My husband was instructed to sit with me as the doctor stitched me up and administered more medication to me.

I woke up fourteen hours later in the recovery room and a nurse came in and told me she was a Christian and had to tell me about my baby, but could we pray first. I was glad for her professionalism and her love for the Father. We are friends to this day! She proceeded to tell me that due to the violent contractions and the dry birth, as well as being breach, the baby had suffered complications. He had a large subdural hematoma on his forehead, which covered forty percent of the cranium. However, I was told that it had not touched the fontanel, which was a good thing. My pelvic bones had literally crushed his head.

The nurse told me I could go see him in an hour after they made sure I was emotionally and medically OK. She also said I should be prepared because due to the hematoma and the circumstances surrounding his birth, he had an eye problem which was currently covered with gauze and would be removed for me to see when they changed the gauze at the next shift. They informed me that he did not breathe on his own after birth because he was eight weeks premature and his lungs lacked a necessary enzyme that signals the lungs to inflate. This enzyme is usually formed in the last six weeks of development. His lungs never inflated so he was currently on a ventilator and on oxygen, which was being pumped inside a "cake pan" which was over and around his head. Monitors were also hooked up to his breathing apparatus as well as electrodes secured to his body in various places.

When they felt I was well enough to see him and able to absorb the information, they wheeled me in to see him. The doctor, I was told, had never left my son's side. In this large room was a nurse, my baby in a large Plexiglas cart filled with medical items, and me. Another nurse came into the room and asked if I wanted to see his eye, as she had to change the bandage so that I could understand what was happening. I nodded yes. She removed the bandage and opened the eyelid for me to see. When I looked, there was no eyeball present that I could recognize as being a human eyeball. It simply looked like a squashed, peeled green grape. They helped me to sit back down in the wheelchair while my doctor stood at the table on the other side of the glass partition. I felt weak. I was told that my husband had already been there and had seen the baby and was presently at work. I had not even realized that it was the next day already. I had not seen the large bruising on the baby's skull at this point. Then, it too was unwrapped, and an ugly bruise the size of a drink coaster, or an almost five-inch oval, was on the side of his head. It covered most of his forehead and eyebrow and went to the crown of his head.

I was wheeled back to my room, checked again and left alone. I cried out to God and told Him that if He wanted to take my son home, it was all right. I believed that God was perfect in all His ways and deep inside I felt that I didn't deserve this child because of all I had done in my past. The nurse came back into the room that had prayed with me before and I asked her if she would pray with me again. She did and told me she would be praying for my baby as well. When she left the room, I picked up the Bible, which seemed to almost open by itself to the Book of Psalms. My eyes fell upon a scripture that seemed to stand out from the rest. It was Psalms 118:17-18. It reads: *"I will not die, but live, and declare the works of the Lord. The Lord hath chastened me sore: but he hath not given me over unto death"* (KJV). I instinctively knew the first verse was for my son and that he would live and be well and that the second verse was for me. I felt that somehow all that was going on would be used for my good and I would grow in Christ and be led to a greater life in Him.

The next morning, my husband and I were both informed that the baby had had trouble breathing and they did not have the proper equipment to sustain his life at our rural hospital. The doctor also asked us for forgiveness and told us that he knew personally how we felt because his own son had been born prematurely and traumatically in another hospital five years earlier, and he understood how incredibly difficult this was for us. We forgave him on the spot.

Our baby was transferred to another hospital in a nearby city where he would receive the rest of his treatment until he was eventually released. They gave us a rather glum picture of his future if he even survived. He would face the possibility of mental retardation, most likely would have many physical difficulties and would suffer blindness in his one eye and probably have very poor vision in the other eye. They told us that *if* his lungs could form the enzyme by themselves and grow and strengthen and he could ever respire on his own...and *if* the X-rays showed his skull bones were healing properly and he could feed on his own and grow, he would be allowed to come home. However, the probability of the enzyme forming post-womb was not likely and there was no artificial enzyme available to cause the lungs to inflate on their own. He was also being watched for signs of brain swelling, which would require emergency surgery along with monitoring of his heart, which the doctors felt was weakened by the lack of oxygen at birth.

I was discharged and went home to an empty room with a baby crib. When my other children went off to school, I would lie on the floor and cry out to God for a miracle. My husband called my doctor, and I was admitted to the hospital for another ten days. I was determined to see God move and would not hide the fact that we would pray until we saw Him perform the miracle He had promised me. Several pastors that we knew kept rounds praying in the neonatal intensive care unit. God provided and the hospital allowed all five pastors to take shifts coming in to pray. On day eleven, my husband and I drove to the neonatal intensive care unit. It was explained to us that our baby was still very ill, but had suddenly on day nine started breathing on his own and was taken off the ventilator. They were monitoring him very closely with just the oxygen tube and measuring his blood gases to see if he was, indeed, getting enough oxygen into his lungs and respiring on his own. He had gained weight, to near normal, being now at almost six pounds. His bruising had disappeared almost entirely and was now the size of a dime. His prognosis was improving daily. The nurse later informed us that it was very unusual, but on day eight, the enzyme necessary to help his lungs breath on their own began to show up in his blood. On day thirteen, he was officially discharged.

We were also told that during the two weeks when we had the prayer vigil going on in the neonatal ward, there were no deaths, which had never happened before. And when they unwrapped his eyes on the morning of the twelfth day, there were two glistening *perfect* eyeballs staring back at them! God had created a new eyeball during the days my son was covered up with bandages! At the end of day thirteen, we were able to take our very small, but breathing son home.

Five months later, the pediatrician told us that our son's skull bones were not moving into position properly to begin the closure that a baby's skull is supposed to make. He informed us that this was the result of his traumatic birth and if these bones did not close, we would be facing the possibility of mental retardation and other developmental problems. A few months later, we were advised to agree to a high-risk surgery to close the bones in his skull, and told that if we chose not to have the surgery, his prognosis was very dire. We shared this with our prayer group who stood with us for the completion of our son's miracle.

Two months later, we received another opinion stating that the baby was fine and that his fontanel seemed to have mildly overlapped a bit near the crown. The doctor stated that there was no danger to the brain and surgery would not be required!

My son is now twenty-four and has overcome every physical challenge he has faced in his body! He even has 20/20 eyesight! He is currently deployed in Kuwait and is due to arrive home this spring! We serve an awesome God!

—Pamela J. Miller

Note from the Author

It has been a blessing for me to put together this book. I would like to say *thank you* to each and every one for sending me their "hope-lift." Each story reminded me of just how big our God is and how faithful He is to meet every one of our needs.

I received hundreds of hope-lifts, but unfortunately I was unable to use all of them. I was tenderly reminded by the Holy Spirit as I put this book together that each testimony represents a person who has been touched by the Father in a significant way, and each life is an expression of His unfailing love for humanity.

My prayer for each of my readers is that in this time when hope is failing, these hope-lifts will renew your faith in God, who is good all the time. We serve a personal God who loves us more than we can comprehend, because He is love! If you have read this book but have never personally met Jesus, He is available to touch your life at the deepest place of your need. He not only loves the people who have sent me their stories, but He loves you as well. He loves you so much that He sent His Son Jesus to die for you over 2,000 years ago on a cross where He took all your sins, all your failures, all your pain on Himself, so that you can be free! If you desire to meet the living God for the first time, please pray this simple prayer:

> Heavenly Father, I thank You for sending Your Son, Jesus, to die for my sins. You know every one of my hurts, my pains, my failures, my sins. I thank You that in spite of everything I have done, You still love me. Please forgive me and make Yourself known to me. In Jesus' name, amen.

If you have just prayed that simple prayer for the first time, let me be the first one to say how excited I am for you! Your life will never be the same! Be sure you find a good church where you live so you can learn more about Jesus.

I would like to thank Carol Bailey for helping me put this book together! I could not have done it without her! Thanks, Carol! You are the best!

All my love,

Ruth Chironna

storiesofhope55@gmail.com

CPSIA information can be obtained
at www.ICGtesting.com
Printed in the USA
LVOW08s0302060318
568708LV00001B/148/P